WISE UP

Books by Kevin Johnson

Early Teen Devotionals

Can I Be a Christian Without Being Weird?
Could Someone Wake Me Up Before I Drool on the Desk?
Does Anybody Know What Planet My Parents Are From?
So Who Says I Have to Act My Age?
Was That a Balloon or Did Your Head Just Pop?
Who Should I Listen To?
Why Can't My Life Be a Summer Vacation?
Why Is God Looking for Friends?

Early Teen Discipleship

Get God: Make Friends With the King of the Universe
Wise Up: Stand Clear of the Unsmartness of Sin
Cross Train: Blast Through the Bible From Front to Back
Pray Hard: Talk to God With Total Confidence

Books for Youth

Catch the Wave!
Find Your Fit[1]
Find Your Fit Discovery Workbook[1]
Find Your Fit Leader's Guide[1]
God's Will, God's Best[2]
Jesus Among Other Gods: Youth Edition[3]
Look Who's Toast Now!
What Do Ya Know?
What's With the Dudes at the Door?[4]
What's With the Mutant in the Microscope?[4]

———————

To find out more about Kevin Johnson's books or speaking availability
visit his Web site: www.thewave.org

[1]with Jane Kise [2]with Josh McDowell [3]with Ravi Zacharias [4]with James White   01A

Stand Clear of the Unsmartness of Sin

WISE UP

Kevin Johnson

BETHANYHOUSE

MINNEAPOLIS, MINNESOTA

Published by Bethany House Publishers
A Ministry of Bethany Fellowship International
11400 Hampshire Avenue South
Bloomington, Minnesota 55438
www.bethanyhouse.com

Printed in the United States of America by
Bethany Press International, Bloomington, Minnesota 55438

Library of Congress Cataloging-in-Publication Data

Johnson, Kevin (Kevin Walter)
    Wise up : stand clear of the unsmartness of sin / by Kevin Johnson.
        p.   cm. — (Early teen discipleship ; 2)
    ISBN 1-55661-637-6
    1. Sin—Biblical teaching—Juvenile literature.   2. Christian teenagers—Religious life—Juvenile literature.   3. Bible—Textbooks. [1. Christian life.   2. Conduct of life.   3. Bible—Study.] I. Title.
    BS680.S57 J64 2000
    248.8'3—dc21
                                                                        00-010397

To

Todd, Sally, Stefan,
Elise, and Julianna

Your friendship is a gift from God

KEVIN JOHNSON is the bestselling author of almost twenty books for youth, including *Can I Be a Christian Without Being Weird?* and *Catch the Wave!* A full-time author and speaker, he served as senior editor for adult nonfiction at Bethany House Publishers and pastored a group of more than four hundred sixth through ninth graders at Elmbrook Church in metro Milwaukee. While his training includes an M.Div. from Fuller Theological Seminary and a B.A. in English and Print Journalism from the University of Wisconsin–River Falls, his current interests include cycling, guitar, and shortwave radio. Kevin and his wife, Lyn, live in Minnesota with their three children—Nate, Karin, and Elise.

Contents

Part 3: Scrubbing Up Your Attitudes

Part 4: Sudsing Up Your Actions

Part 5: Standing Up to Sin

How to Use This Book

Welcome to *Wise Up*. This book is part of the EARLY TEEN DISCIPLESHIP series, better remembered by its clever initials, ETD. I wrote ETD as a follow-up to my series of bestselling devotionals—books like *Can I Be a Christian Without Being Weird?* and *Could Someone Wake Me Up Before I Drool on the Desk?* ETD has one aim: to help you take your next step in becoming wildly devoted to Jesus. If you're ready to work on a vital, heart-to-heart, sold-out relationship with God, this is your series.

The goal of *this* book, *Wise Up*, is to help you get close to God and stand clear of the unsmartness of sin. *Wise Up* prods you toward that goal through twenty-five Bible studies designed to make you think—okay, without *totally* breaking your brain. It will help you

- dig into Scripture on your own
- feed on insights that you might not otherwise find
- hit the heart issues that push you away from God or pull you closer to him.

You can pick your own pace—anything from a study a day to a study a week. But here's what you'll find in each study:

- Your first stop is BRAIN DRAIN—your spot at the beginning of each lesson to spout what you think.
- Then there's FLASHBACK—a bit of background so you better understand what's coming up.
- Don't skip over the BIBLE CHUNK—a hand-picked Bible passage to read.
- You get STUFF TO KNOW—questions to help you dig into what a passage means.
- There's INSIGHT—facts about the passage you might not figure out on your own.
- DA'SCOOP—definitions of weird words.
- And SIDELIGHT—other Bible verses that let you see the topic from a different angle.

The other big questions are, well . . .

- BIG QUESTIONS—your chance to apply what you have learned to your life.
- Each study wraps up with a DEEP THOT—a thought to chew on.

  But that's not the end.

- There's STICKY STUFF—a Bible verse to jam into your brain juice.
- ACT ON IT—a way to do something with what you just learned.
- And DIG ON—another Bible passage to unearth if you want more.

And one more thing: There are cards in the back of the book for all the verses in STICKY STUFF, with a few bonus cards thrown in—since we'd already killed the tree.

If you've got a pencil and know how to use it, you're all set.

EXCEPT FOR ONE THING You can study
Wise Up on your own. But you can also work through this book with a friend or in a group. After every five studies there's a page called "Talk About It." Nope—you don't have to cover every question on the page. There are too many to answer, so pick the ones that matter most to you.

Whenever you do an ETD study with one friend or a bunch, keep in mind three goals—and three big questions to help you remember those goals. And nope—you don't have to actually ask those questions each time, because that would feel canned. But each time you meet you want to

- EMPATHIZE: *What's gone on since the last time you got together?* To "empathize" means to put yourself in someone else's shoes. Galatians 6:2 tells us to "carry each other's burdens" (NIV), or to "share each other's troubles and problems" (NLT). Whether you call them "highs and lows," "wows and pows," "uppers and downers," or "wins and wedgies," take time to celebrate and support each other by chatting through life's important happenings and offering simple, to-the-point prayers.
- ENCOURAGE: *Where are you at with Jesus?* Hebrews 3:13 says to "encourage one another daily. . . so that none of you may be hardened by sin's deceitfulness." Religious rules apart from a relationship with God are deadly. So instead be real: Are you

growing closer to or wandering away from the Lord you're learning to follow? Is anything tripping you up?

- EQUIP: *What one truth are you going to take away from today that will help you live closer to Jesus?* Second Timothy 3:16–17 promises that "All Scripture is inspired by God and is useful to teach us what is true and to make us realize what is wrong in our lives. It straightens us out and teaches us to do what is right. It is God's way of preparing us in every way, fully equipped for every good thing God wants us to do" (NLT). Don't leave your get-together without one point of truth that will make a difference in your life. It might not be the thought or verse that anyone else picks. But grab at least one truth—and hang on tight by letting it make a difference in your life.

Got it? Not only is *Wise Up* a study to do on your own, but better yet, it can help you grow your faith with your friends. You can pick a leader—a youth or adult—or take turns picking questions and talking through them as your time allows. Just keep the three big goals in mind.

Now you're ready. You can do it. Grow ahead and turn the page and get started.

PART 1

THE WAY OF THE WISE

1. The Body-Sized Blender
Wanting God's wise way

You hurdle up and over a barbed-wire fence sporting a big KEEP OUT sign. You shimmy on your belly across a runway. You scoot past security guards meant to shoo you to safety. And then you ignore the simple yet bold warning on the side of a plane—a sticker that politely maps the cone of death in front of the jet engines, the zone where the whirring turbines suck in anything that steps too close. You'd thought the best way to understand a jet engine was to get an up-close look. So now you're getting an up-close look, all right—like seeing the inside of a body-sized blender.

BRAIN DRAIN What's the *dumbest* thing you've ever done and lived to tell about? Ever fallen out of a tree? Slammed your hand in a car door? Put something in your ear smaller than your elbow?

FLASHBACK Life is full of "Don't-run-with-scissors" or "Stay-away-from-jet-engines" kind of rules—nuggets of wisdom that may or may not keep you from bodily harm. The Bible's wisdom is even bigger than the kind of smarts that keep you from putting a sharp stick in your eye. It's wisdom that helps you stick close to God and stand clear of the unsmartness of sin. This Bible Chunk is all about why you would *want* to wise up.

BIBLE CHUNK Read Proverbs 2:1–11

(1) My son, if you accept my words
    and store up my commands within you,

(2) turning your ear to wisdom
  and applying your heart to understanding,
(3) and if you call out for insight
  and cry aloud for understanding,
(4) and if you look for it as for silver
  and search for it as for hidden treasure,
(5) then you will understand the fear of the Lord
  and find the knowledge of God.
(6) For the Lord gives wisdom,
  and from his mouth come knowledge and understanding.
(7) He holds victory in store for the upright,
  he is a shield to those whose walk is blameless,
(8) for he guards the course of the just
  and protects the way of his faithful ones.
(9) Then you will understand what is right and just
  and fair—every good path.
(10) For wisdom will enter your heart,
  and knowledge will be pleasant to your soul.
(11) Discretion will protect you,
  and understanding will guard you.

STUFF TO KNOW There's a whole heap of "ifs" at
the beginning of that Chunk. What are they? Scribble them down
or circle them. (If you count all the phrases in verses 1–4, you
should find eight.)

All those "ifs" sound like a lot of work. But what do you get if you
search hard for wisdom (verse 5)?

Puzzled? You're maybe thinking you're not thrilled about getting
knowledge. You're probably pretty sure you don't want fear. But
whose wisdom are you guaranteed to get (verse 6)?

INSIGHT "Fear of the Lord" can be either healthy or horri-
fying. Think of the healthy kind as the utter respect you should

rightly have for God, the King of the Universe. And the knowledge you get from God is the kind of jaw-dropping, awe-inspiring, life-changing wisdom you would expect from someone who is not only all-powerful but all-knowing and all-kind. Proverbs 1:7 says, "The fear of the Lord [or "respect for the Lord"] is the beginning of knowledge, but fools despise wisdom and discipline."

So what good is God's wisdom? Why wise up? List a bunch of reasons from verses 7–10, and circle two that sound best to you.

BIG QUESTIONS When has a warning—from a friend, parent, teacher, or stranger—helped you?

How would a sign that tells you how to avoid getting sliced and diced by a jet engine be "pleasant knowledge"?

Do you think God shares his wisdom to wreck your life—or to make it wildly enjoyable? Why do you think that?

SIDELIGHT If you have any doubt about God's good goals for you, ponder a couple Bible Chunks. God once spoke through the prophet Jeremiah and said, "I know the plans I have for you . . . plans to prosper you and not to harm you, plans to give you hope and a future" (Jeremiah 29:11). And Jesus put it this way: "I have come that they may have life, and have it to the full" (John 10:10).

How helpful do you think God's wisdom could be to you? How would it lead you into "every good path" (verse 9)? How is it "pleasant" (verse 10)? How might it "protect you" (verse 11)?

So how important do you think it is to wise up by getting God's smarts?

SIDELIGHT Here's an angle on the importance of gaining wisdom you might not have thought of. As an adult, Jesus often astonished people with his sharp insights (see places like Mark 6:1–5 and Matthew 11:19). But even more astounding is the fact that Jesus had been wise all along. As a little kid Jesus "was filled with wisdom" (Luke 2:40). Wising up was so important to Jesus that the Bible boils down his childhood to two things: He grew up and he grew wise. And as a result he had the favor of both God and people (Luke 2:52).

DEEP THOT God's wisdom is what keeps you from hitting the big fan of life. God wants you to wise up so you can stand clear of the unsmartness of sin. It's the only way you can experience the good life he intends for you.

STICKY STUFF Wise up by memorizing Proverbs 2:6. There's a removable card in the back to help you out.

ACT IT OUT Ask an adult "So who was the smartest person you ever knew?" What kind of smarts did he or she have? How did those smarts show?

DIG ON Read Proverbs 1 for a bunch more reasons why God's wisdom is what you want to get.

2. Sippin' From the Stream
Sticking close to God

Jason hadn't ever tried to hide the fact that he followed Jesus. Now he was wondering if he should have. A few kids thought Jason's faith was cool. Most people ignored it as just another thing he was into—like video games and hockey. But almost every day now, the kid with the locker next to Jason's kept saying Jason was too chicken to try anything else. Too girly to grow up. And—above all— too stupid to think for himself. Jason was beginning to think maybe his faith wasn't so smart after all.

BRAIN DRAIN What does having a relationship with God do for you? What's good about it? What's bad?

FLASHBACK Think hard about the first word in this Bible Chunk—"blessed"—because it describes everything good that comes after it. While you might think "blessed" is a word fit only to slip from the lips of a saintly old grandma, in the Bible "blessed" actually means "happy." Yet it isn't a fleeting feeling. It's a deep peace and satisfaction. In other words, being "blessed" isn't gaggy. It's good. It's what wising up God's way is all about.

BIBLE CHUNK Read Psalm 1

(1) Blessed is the man
   who does not walk in the counsel of the wicked
or stand in the way of sinners

nor sit in the seat of mockers.
(2) But his delight is in the law of the Lord,
and on his law he meditates day and night.
(3) He is like a tree planted by streams of water,
which yields its fruit in season
and whose leaf does not wither.
Whatever he does prospers.
(4) Not so the wicked!
They are like chaff
that the wind blows away.
(5) Therefore the wicked will not stand in the judgment,
nor sinners in the assembly of the righteous.
(6) For the Lord watches over the way of the righteous,
but the way of the wicked will perish.

STUFF TO KNOW Psalm 1 says a certain type of person is blessed. From verses 1–3, scribble down five things you know about a blessed person:

INSIGHT Some people see stages of badness at the beginning of this Bible Chunk, as in someone first stumbling, then splattering on the ground, and finally getting stuck in muck. To live according to the counsel of the wacked-out—that's plenty bad. To hang tight with sinners—that's worse yet. And to grab a seat with people who mock God—that's getting cemented in sin. The bigger point, though, is that a guy or gal wise to God's ways avoids *all* of that.

While people who are wicked, sinful, and cynical are doing their thing, what is the person blessed by God doing (verse 2)?

DA'SCOOP In Hebrew, the language in which this Bible Chunk was originally written, "meditate" literally means "mutter." Back then people seldom had access to written Scripture. So they memorized passages and continually rolled them around in their

brains. It's still a great way to stay stuffed full of God's wisdom.

What happens to people who choose to wise up by pondering God's words? What is he or she like (verse 3)?

INSIGHT Don't forget that this psalm wasn't written by someone sipping iced cappuccino by a pool. It comes from arid Israel. The point? God's followers aren't like stunted trees that grow wild in desert rocks. They don't trust luck to get occasional sprinkles of rain. God's followers are like trees planted next to a stream—or, actually, an irrigation ditch. They lap up regular, reliable refreshment sent their way by their Planter.

What will happen to people who don't follow God (verses 4–6)?

BIG QUESTIONS Of all the people in your world— peers, parents, big personalities, teachers, brothers and sisters— who defines what is "smart"? How much do they agree with the Bible—or not?

Do you think God's wisdom is worth "delighting" in, like it says in verse 2? Why or why not?

Think about what Psalm 1 says happens to the blessed. Then study what happens to the wicked. Hmmm . . . which way of living sounds smart to you?

How would your life be different if you stuck close to God's stream—in other words, if you continually learned from God and totally lived out what you know?

What keeps you from giving God your wild, wholehearted obedience? What *doesn't* sound smart about gulping from the stream?

That brings up the big question: Is wising up and living God's way what you're looking for? Why or why not?

DEEP THOT Because God made you, you are already uniquely valuable. Because of Jesus' death for you on the cross, you are already acceptable to God. But if you don't stick close to God and live his way, you still aren't living smart. God wants to plop you by the stream of his life-giving wisdom. If you choose to, you can drink up—and wise up.

STICKY STUFF Be like the Bible folks who muttered to themselves about God's wisdom by memorizing Psalm 1:1–2. It will help you remember what's truly smart.

ACT ON IT At the beginning of this Bible Chunk the blessed person might sound like a solo act. But verse 5 says there's an "assembly" of people who follow God. Find someone who can study *Wise Up* with you.

DIG ON Ever wonder why nasty people don't always blow away in the breeze? Check out Psalm 73 for some insight into the real fate of evildoers—and God's real care for his people.

3. Where Smarts Come From

God's flawless wisdom

Kaitlin shivered at the thought of a technician slicing open her head—until the salesperson convinced her of the advantages of broadband Internet access wired straight into her brain. Sure, she'd have to connect to a terminal via nerve implants in her hand—a little like sticking her finger in a light socket—because her parents wouldn't splurge for wireless. But hey, as long as she's plugged in, she'd be the biggest brain in the world. Or so she thought.

BRAIN DRAIN If you could hard-wire your brain directly into any one source of information on the planet, what would it be?

FLASHBACK You can tap an ultrahuge world of human knowledge on the Net. But you don't need to go ultra-hi-tech to tap into God. Psalm 19 tells how you can access the ultimate smarts in the universe—right here, right now, with no surgical fuss or muss.

BIBLE CHUNK Read Psalm 19

(1) The heavens declare the glory of God;
   the skies proclaim the work of his hands.
(2) Day after day they pour forth speech;
   night after night they display knowledge.
(3) There is no speech or language
   where their voice is not heard.

(4) Their voice goes out into all the earth,
  their words to the ends of the world.
In the heavens he has pitched a tent for the sun,
    (5) which is like a bridegroom coming forth from his pavilion,
    like a champion rejoicing to run his course.
(6) It rises at one end of the heavens
    and makes its circuit to the other;
    nothing is hidden from its heat.
(7) The law of the Lord is perfect,
    reviving the soul.
The statutes of the Lord are trustworthy,
    making wise the simple.
(8) The precepts of the Lord are right,
    giving joy to the heart.
The commands of the Lord are radiant,
    giving light to the eyes.
(9) The fear of the Lord is pure,
    enduring forever.
The ordinances of the Lord are sure
    and altogether righteous.
(10) They are more precious than gold,
    than much pure gold;
    they are sweeter than honey,
    than honey from the comb.
(11) By them is your servant warned;
    in keeping them there is great reward.
(12) Who can discern his errors?
    Forgive my hidden faults.
(13) Keep your servant also from willful sins;
    may they not rule over me.
Then will I be blameless,
    innocent of great transgression.
(14) May the words of my mouth and the meditation of my heart
    be pleasing in your sight,
O Lord, my Rock and my Redeemer.

STUFF TO KNOW Psalm 19 says there are two ways to access info about who God is and how he wants us to live. What are they? (Hint: You can spot the first in verse 1. Look for the second in verses 7–9.)

You can see God's wisdom both in his *works*, the things he's made, and in his *words*, the things he says. What does *creation* tell you about God (verse 1)?

What kinds of things do God's *words* tell you (verses 7–11)?

Those things—like "laws," "statutes," "precepts," and "commands"—sound scary. But what is David's attitude toward God's words (verses 7–11)?

SIDELIGHT The Bible book of Romans points out that God's *work* of creation shows humans enough about God that we are "without excuse." We can tell that God put us here, that we belong to him, and that we answer to him (Romans 1:19–20). But God has also spoken in *words*, first through his prophets (2 Peter 1:19–22) and then through Jesus. He is *the* Word, God fully on display (John 1:1–14). The Bible wraps together all of God's words for you to read firsthand. Unlike any other source of knowledge, the Bible tells you how to get to God through Jesus and shows you God's wise way to live (2 Timothy 3:15–16).

What happens when you tap into the wisdom of God's words? Name the four things in verses 7 and 8 that God's words do for you.

BIG QUESTIONS Have you ever used the Bible to

wise up? How? Is it easy or hard—or interesting or boring—for you to read?

Name a person you know who uses the Bible to figure out how to live. Why does he or she trust the Bible?

How do the smarts that person gains from the Bible make a difference in real life?

How do *you* want to use God's words to wise up?

DEEP THOT Nothing on earth can match God's infinite intelligence. He knows everything about your world—and about you. If you want to wise up, then grab hold of what he wants to teach you through his works and his words.

STICKY STUFF Do a nonsurgical implant of Psalm 19:7 in your neural network. Or you can just memorize it. Either way.

ACT ON IT Set a goal for how many Bible verses you want to permanently fix in your head while reading *Wise Up*. There's one in the "Sticky Stuff" section of each chapter.

DIG ON Psalm 119 is the longest chapter in the Bible—and it happens to be all about the greatness of God's words. Give it a read.

(4.) Scratch and Sniff
Wising up changes how you live

"They're really spiritual!" Jolene gushed about her new friends. "It's like they can smell sin. They take one whiff of you and they know everything you've ever done wrong." Jolene wanted to drag Cassie to meet these friends, but Cassie wasn't thrilled about being treated like a spiritual scratch and sniff. Jolene's friends might be really mature, Cassie thought—but then again, they sounded more spooky than spiritual. Cassie wasn't so sure that being able to detect ugly odors in someone else's life was what being a Christian was all about.

BRAIN DRAIN Describe the most mature Christian you know. Better yet, draw a tiny picture in the space below. Label key parts.

FLASHBACK Just before this Bible Chunk, Paul—the author of this letter to believers at Ephesus, a city in what is now Turkey—wrote that when you come to know Jesus, you don't live like you used to—but you also don't become a sin-sniffing snob. In this Bible Chunk he explains that wising up causes two huge things to happen: You imitate God, and you live as a child of light. And at the end he nails this point: Becoming wise causes you to watch how you live.

BIBLE CHUNK Read Ephesians 5:1–16

(1) Be imitators of God, therefore, as dearly loved children (2) and live a life of love, just as Christ loved us and gave himself up for us as a fragrant offering and sacrifice to God.

(3) But among you there must not be even a hint of sexual immorality, or of any kind of impurity, or of greed, because these are improper for God's holy people. (4) Nor should there be obscenity, foolish talk or coarse joking, which are out of place, but rather thanksgiving. (5) For of this you can be sure: No immoral, impure or greedy person—such a man is an idolater—has any inheritance in the kingdom of Christ and of God. (6) Let no one deceive you with empty words, for because of such things God's wrath comes on those who are disobedient. (7) Therefore do not be partners with them.

(8) For you were once darkness, but now you are light in the Lord. Live as children of light (9) (for the fruit of the light consists in all goodness, righteousness and truth) (10) and find out what pleases the Lord. (11) Have nothing to do with the fruitless deeds of darkness, but rather expose them. (12) For it is shameful even to mention what the disobedient do in secret. (13) But everything exposed by the light becomes visible, (14) for it is light that makes everything visible. This is why it is said:

"Wake up, O sleeper,
rise from the dead,
and Christ will shine on you."

(15) Be very careful, then, how you live—not as unwise but as wise, (16) making the most of every opportunity, because the days are evil.

STUFF TO KNOW What does it mean to "live a life of love"? Actually, that question has three parts. Part one: Who should you imitate (verse 1)?

Part two: Who is your giant example of what love is? What did he do for you (verse 2)?

Part three: What does that "life of love" look like? How would you act if you were doing an imitation of God (verses 3–5)?

INSIGHT Do you see it? Getting wise brings concrete results. When you start to grow as a Christian, God rearranges your love life—how you act toward others, especially the opposite sex.

He does a make-over of your mouth—how you speak to others. And he teaches you to crown Jesus King of your life. Lots of people make loads of other things sound highly spiritual. But a life of love—based on Christ's example, impacting the most basic areas of life—is what wisdom is all about.

There's another description of the Christian life in verse 8. What is it? Christians are to live loving lives, doing an imitation of God. How else do they live (verse 8)?

When we live as children of light, whom do we please (verse 10)?

INSIGHT When you walk in the light—when you wise up and live as God commands—you won't stumble around wondering about right and wrong. You start to see where you are going. You begin to understand what pleases God. And you ditch evil, the kind of living that ignores the wisdom of God's command. This Bible Chunk calls that type of life "fruitless deeds of darkness" (verse 11).

So what are you supposed to do about evil (verses 11–14)?

INSIGHT Mixed-up here? This Bible Chunk seems to say two different things: (1) "expose evil," yet (2) "don't talk about evil." The way to overcome evil isn't to yammer endlessly about bad things people do but to choose for yourself to live out God's commands. But when you do the right thing, it sometimes becomes obvious that other people are doing the wrong thing. God's light shines on you, and you reflect it into dark places. The light of your life—often with no words necessary—shows darkness for what it is. So without hunting for evil you still expose it.

BIG QUESTIONS Hmmm . . . imitating God. That's a big order—unless you're a chip off the ol' block. How can you "live a life of love" like God does? Think hard about verse 2.

You can live a life of love—or a life of light—when you bask in the love of Christ, who gave himself for you by dying on the cross. So how might people react if you live like that?

INSIGHT When you live like light your friends might appreciate you about as much as a flashlight beamed right in their eyes. They might think you're a sin-sniffer—whether you intend that or not. You need the info and encouragement in verses 15–16: Wise up, make your own good choices, and take advantage of opportunities to share God's love.

DEEP THOT When you wise up—and decide to live by that wisdom—you get a new life. You imitate God. You reflect God's light. You can't wise up without people noticing. But getting smart is about changing you—not showing off to others.

STICKY STUFF Be careful. Put Ephesians 5:15 in your brain.

ACT ON IT Practice imitating God and living as a child of light—but keep track of times you turn into a sin-sniffer.

DIG ON Look at what John 3:16–21 says about how people reacted to the light of Jesus.

⑤ Caveman Re-creation
Getting to know God remakes you

When it was Brandon's turn to talk at the campfire, he looked down and dug his toe in the dirt. After a few days out in the woods with his church friends, he had some stuff to get out. "You guys know I've always been to church," he said. "But usually I don't know what's going on. When the rest of you talk about being friends with Jesus, I don't know what you mean. Church is just a bunch of rules to me. I do stuff I know I shouldn't. I also know I'm in trouble more than I want to be. I'd really like to have what you have."

BRAIN DRAIN If you had a friend who was acting less-than-wise and not sure about how God could help, what would you say to her or him?

FLASHBACK Know what? Merely knowing the right thing to do never made anyone do it. We might want to live wisely. We might want to stand clear of sin. But how? There's only one real answer: Jesus. And the letter that Paul wrote to his friend Titus tells how to get started. See, Titus was on a Mediterranean island called Crete, aiming to help the Cretans wise up. One problem: Cretans had a reputation for being dumb as stumps. In fact, calling someone a "cretan" was more or less saying he was a slope-foreheaded caveman. But check out how God could help even those unibrows.

BIBLE CHUNK Read Titus 3:1–8

(1) Remind the people to be subject to rulers and authorities, to be obedient, to be ready to do whatever is good, (2) to slander no one, to be

peaceable and considerate, and to show true humility toward all men. (3) At one time we too were foolish, disobedient, deceived and enslaved by all kinds of passions and pleasures. We lived in malice and envy, being hated and hating one another. (4) But when the kindness and love of God our Savior appeared, (5) he saved us, not because of righteous things we had done, but because of his mercy. He saved us through the washing of rebirth and renewal by the Holy Spirit, (6) whom he poured out on us generously through Jesus Christ our Savior, (7) so that, having been justified by his grace, we might become heirs having the hope of eternal life. (8) This is a trustworthy saying. And I want you to stress these things, so that those who have trusted in God may be careful to devote themselves to doing what is good. These things are excellent and profitable for everyone.

STUFF TO KNOW What was Titus supposed to remind the Cretans to do—or not do (verses 1–2)?

That's what the Cretans are supposed to look like—but at the moment, that's not where they were at. When Paul says, "Hey, we were all once like . . ." what does that imply the Cretans are like? List a bunch of ugly things the Cretans must have seen when they looked in a mirror (verse 3).

Paul wasn't picking on the Cretans. He's willing to admit he was once a spiritual slob. So what changed Paul (verses 4–7)?

Hang on tight—because thinking through these verses bit by bit reveals some gargantuan, life-changing factoids. Exactly who kindly reaches into our lives and changes us (verses 4–5)?

What did we do to earn "the kindness and love of God our Savior" (verse 5)?

SIDELIGHT The fact that God loves us just as we are is one of the Bible's most astounding truths. The best-known Bible verse on this topic is Romans 5:8: "But God demonstrates his own love for us in this: While we were still sinners, Christ died for us." God doesn't "save" us—make us friends with him and make us new—because we deserve his favor. He chooses to love us even when we are unlovable.

This Bible Chunk next strings together a whole Chunk of things that happen when Jesus is your Savior. What are they (verses 5–7)?

In a second we'll get to what all those things mean. But once we trust God, what are we able to do (verse 8)?

INSIGHT First Corinthians 1:30 says that Jesus "has become for us wisdom from God." If you want to truly get wise, you need to get Jesus. If you want to stand clear of the unsmartness of sin, you need to stick close to him.

    It's like this: When you become a Christian—when God saves you—two major things happen. First, you're *reborn* spiritually—made God's child. You're washed clean of your sins—forgiven. You're justified—made right in God's sight. Second, you start to *grow*. You get a new life that starts now and lasts for eternity. God starts some fantastic changes in you—that's the "renewal by the Holy Spirit." And that new relationship with God is what makes it possible for you to become the wise person God wants you to be.

BIG QUESTIONS This Bible Chunk lays out *the facts of what God has done for us*. Other Bible Chunks emphasize *our right response to these facts*. We have all done wrong against God. We've all wrecked up our relationship with him to the point that we deserve death—eternal separation from him. We are, however, made right with God when we accept those facts. In some spots the Bible calls that "having faith" (Romans 3:22–26). In Titus 3:8 it's called "trusting in God." So—really big question—do you trust in God? What does that mean to you?

You might have grown up trusting in God. You maybe remember a specific time and place where you decided you believed in him. But you can also get started on that relationship with God right now. Here's how you truly wise up. You can tell God, "God, I've done wrong against you. I know that Jesus died in my place for those wrongs—those sins. I accept the forgiveness you can offer me because of his death for me. And I want to live wisely for you." Believe that? Then grow on.

DEEP THOT God can even re-create Cretan cavemen. But getting to know him is the only way it happens.

STICKY STUFF Hang on tight to Titus 3:4–5. It's all about how God hangs on to you.

ACT ON IT Tell someone what it means to you to have a relationship with God.

DIG ON Check out Colossians 1:21–23 for a tight description of the facts on what it means to trust in God.

Talk About It • 1

EMPATHIZE: What's going on in your life?
ENCOURAGE: How are you doing with Jesus?
EQUIP: What one truth will you take home today?

- When has a warning—from a friend, parent, teacher, stranger—helped you? (Study 1)
- Do you think God shares his wisdom to wreck your life—or to make it wildly enjoyable? Why do you think that? (Study 1)
- What does having a relationship with God do for you? What are the pros and cons? (Study 2)
- What makes a person "blessed" or happy? (Study 2)
- Of all the people in your world—peers, parents, big personalities, teachers, brothers, and sisters—who defines what's smart? How much do they agree with the Bible—or not? (Study 2)
- How do you tap into info about who God is and how he wants you to live? (Study 3)
- Do you want to set a goal of how many "Sticky Stuffs" you want to memorize as you work through Wise Up? (Study 3)
- How does becoming wise cause you to watch how you live? (Study 3)
- What would you look like if you were doing an imitation of God? (Study 4)
- If you had a friend who was acting less-than-smart and not sure about how God could help, what would you say to him or her? (Study 5)
- How does God reach into your life and change you? (Study 5)

PART 2

UNDER CONSTRUCTION

6. Save the Soap
God scrubs you from the inside out

You clapped your hands over your mouth the moment the cuss word crashed past your lips. You fumed. You'd done it again! #@&%*! And there you did it *again*! You pressed your hands over your mouth even harder, letting go only when you stood at the bathroom sink. You'd heard your grandpa tell how his mother washed his mouth out with soap whenever he said a bad word. Sure, Great-Grandma used bar soap, but a squirt of liquid soap on your toothbrush should have the same effect. No, you weren't sure it would help your swearing habit. No, you hadn't thought what the soap might do to your innards. But if it was good enough for your great-grandma, it was good enough for you. . . .

BRAIN DRAIN What do you do when you want to get rid of evil in your life?

FLASHBACK You've already read the Bible Chunk that follows this passage, Ephesians 5:1–16. You saw that when you get to know Jesus, you don't live like you used to. Becoming wise makes you watch how you live. But in this Bible Chunk you back up and see exactly *how* Jesus changes you. He's concerned about your outsides—your actions—but he knows his biggest job is rearranging the attitudes that affect how you act. In this study—and the next four—you'll see *how* God changes you.

BIBLE CHUNK Read Ephesians 4:17–32

(17) So I tell you this, and insist on it in the Lord, that you must no longer live as the Gentiles do, in the futility of their thinking. (18) They are

darkened in their understanding and separated from the life of God because of the ignorance that is in them due to the hardening of their hearts. (19) Having lost all sensitivity, they have given themselves over to sensuality so as to indulge in every kind of impurity, with a continual lust for more.

(20) You, however, did not come to know Christ that way. (21) Surely you heard of him and were taught in him in accordance with the truth that is in Jesus. (22) You were taught, with regard to your former way of life, to put off your old self, which is being corrupted by its deceitful desires; (23) to be made new in the attitude of your minds; (24) and to put on the new self, created to be like God in true righteousness and holiness.

(25) Therefore each of you must put off falsehood and speak truthfully to his neighbor, for we are all members of one body. (26) "In your anger do not sin": Do not let the sun go down while you are still angry, (27) and do not give the devil a foothold. (28) He who has been stealing must steal no longer, but must work, doing something useful with his own hands, that he may have something to share with those in need.

(29) Do not let any unwholesome talk come out of your mouths, but only what is helpful for building others up according to their needs, that it may benefit those who listen. (30) And do not grieve the Holy Spirit of God, with whom you were sealed for the day of redemption. (31) Get rid of all bitterness, rage and anger, brawling and slander, along with every form of malice. (32) Be kind and compassionate to one another, forgiving each other, just as in Christ God forgave you.

STUFF TO KNOW In this Bible Chunk the term "Gentile" refers to people who don't know God. What's wrong with the thinking of people who aren't friends with God (verses 17–18)?

Exactly *why* is their thinking so messed up (verse 18)?

If you're wondering what "hardening of their hearts" is all about, verse 19 explains it. What makes people so thick toward God?

If that's how pagans think, what's different about people who know Christ? Look for one-word answers to three quick questions:

- Whose truth rearranges their brains (verse 21)?
- What type of desires do they ditch (verse 22)?
- What kind of attitudes do they receive (verse 23)?

And what's the result when their minds are remade with God's wisdom? What do they do (verse 24)?

SIDELIGHT
Jesus cut up the religious teachers of his day because they used brute force to discipline their outsides while letting sin run wild on their insides. He said they were like freshly painted tombs—pretty on the surface but full of dead people's bones underneath. He said, "You clean the outside of the cup and dish, but inside [you] are full of greed and self-indulgence. Blind Pharisee! First clean the inside of the cup and dish, and then the outside also will be clean" (Matthew 23:25–26). He also told them that their rotten words, for example, came from rotten innards, and that good words come from a good heart (Matthew 12:34–35).

BIG QUESTIONS
When you have a bad habit to break or some sin that snags you over and over, how have you handled it?

INSIGHT
When you want to change God's way, you can't ignore the "inside of the cup." Maybe you constantly say "God!" in a way that isn't exactly prayerful. You can ask a friend to grab your lips and twist every time you "misuse God's name" (Exodus 20:7). Or you could wash the cup both inside and out by

- thinking about what it means to respect God
- asking God to help you hate wrong and love right
- telling God you want to understand and respect the specialness of his name AND
- asking a friend to poke you when you mess up without thinking.

Verses 25–32 of this Bible Chunk describe the great results you get when you "put off the old self" and "put on the new self," when you ditch not just ungodly behaviors but the thickheaded thinking behind them.

So what things have you tried to change just by gnawing at the outside, like a bad-mouthed boy biting a bar of soap?

How can you scrub not just at the outside of that problem—but at the inside too?

DEEP THOT Sin is something that mucks you up on the inside. That's where God wants to scrub you clean.

STICKY STUFF Wash up with Ephesians 4:23–24.

ACT ON IT Think about a bad habit you have. For every "outside" way you try to change, think of two "inside" ways to attack the problem.

DIG ON Read in Matthew 23 how Jesus laid into the religious leaders for their hypocritical way of wising up.

7. Twisting on a Spit
God's power to change

Mr. Kent leaned forward in his chair. And then he jabbed his finger at Steve's chest. "If you don't make my Ryan feel more welcome in this youth group, you won't be youth pastor at this church much longer. I swear it!" Steve twisted in his chair like a kabob roasting on a barbecue. But then Steve decided he had a point to make of his own. "You know, Mr. Kent, Ryan can quote the Bible backward and forward," he said calmly, "but he isn't very kind. If you saw half of what Ryan does to other kids in the group, you would realize your son has a problem. After all, being a Christian isn't just about what you know. It's about who you are."

BRAIN DRAIN What would you be like if you got really smart about spiritual stuff—but never actually applied it to your life?

FLASHBACK Real wisdom never resides just in your brain. In the Bible, genuine wisdom always makes a difference in your daily life. When wisdom gets into your head, love gets into your heart. First Corinthians 13:2 says you might be able to "fathom all mysteries and all knowledge," but if you don't have love, *you are nothing.* This Bible Chunk highlights all the things God wants to build into you to make you mature.

BIBLE CHUNK Read 2 Peter 1:3–9

(3) His divine power has given us everything we need for life and godliness through our knowledge of him who called us by his own glory and

goodness. (4) Through these he has given us his very great and precious promises, so that through them you may participate in the divine nature and escape the corruption in the world caused by evil desires.

(5) For this very reason, make every effort to add to your faith goodness; and to goodness, knowledge; (6) and to knowledge, self-control; and to self-control, perseverance; and to perseverance, godliness; (7) and to godliness, brotherly kindness; and to brotherly kindness, love. (8) For if you possess these qualities in increasing measure, they will keep you from being ineffective and unproductive in your knowledge of our Lord Jesus Christ. (9) But if anyone does not have them, he is nearsighted and blind, and has forgotten that he has been cleansed from his past sins.

STUFF TO KNOW What has God's power given you (verse 3)?

And how does God give you those things (verse 3)?

INSIGHT When God calls you "by his own glory and goodness," it means that growing you spiritually is something *he* has committed to do. You don't have to beg him. You don't have to bug him. In fact, he's already giving you the "knowledge of him" and the "great and precious promises" you need to grow.

What will God's promises help you do (verse 4)?

INSIGHT "Escaping corruption" means you avoid getting sucked in to the bad attitudes and actions of people around you. "Participating in the divine nature" means God will empower you and shape you to look like him.

So what does a grown-up, wildly wise Christian look like? What qualities would you have (verses 5–7)?

DA'SCOOP Knowing God and grabbing hold of his promises produces change—life-long, full-blown transformation. Your starting point is

- faith (the trust in God that begins when you first believe).

But God wants to build into you all sorts more:

- goodness (moral excellence)
- knowledge (an understanding of God and his plans for you)
- self-control (the capacity to resist doing wrong)
- perseverance (the ability to press on in your faith even when it's hard)
- godliness (paying attention to God in every part of life)
- brotherly kindness (fellowship between God's followers)
- love (sacrificing for others).

What's the result if you keep growing these qualities (verse 8)?

What are you if you *don't* possess those things? What have you forgotten (verse 9)?

BIG QUESTIONS When you look at that list of ways God wants to grow you, where would you like to grow first—and most?

Would you be disappointed if a year from now you realized you didn't know God any better—or trust him any more deeply? Why or why not?

INSIGHT Being "ineffective" and "unproductive" sounds

like no big deal—like at school you maybe didn't do enough extra credit to rocket a grade into the stratosphere. But blowing off God's assignment to grow has results worse than that—the kind of crash-and-burn spiritual life you don't want:

- Feeling distant from God
- Having a spiritual life that seems pointless
- Never experiencing the coolness of living close to God
- Being bored out of your brain in church
- Always wondering if you're really a Christian

DEEP THOT You don't get spiritually smart for the sake of being smart. Knowledge of God is meant to remake your life. It's how you live right and stick close to your Savior.

STICKY STUFF Want to understand how God wants to help you grow? Roll 2 Peter 1:3 around in your head.

ACT ON IT Find an adult—a youth pastor, parent, mentor—who is interested in your long-term spiritual growth. Talk together about how he or she can help you build your faith.

DIG ON Verse 9 says that if you don't want to grow spiritually, you've maybe forgotten you've been forgiven. Jesus once pointed out that one of his followers—a former prostitute—was greatly devoted to him because she knew the ghastliness of her sins. But "he who has been forgiven little," Jesus said, "loves little." It's not that your sins have to be ghastly for you to be grateful. Those of us who think we're "pretty good" need to recall that in God's eyes all sin is really bad. Read Luke 7:36–50 to learn how remembering where you came from—and what God has done for you—grows an attitude of gratitude.

8. Walking Zombies
The Spirit grows fruit in you

Trees do what they're made to do. They suck water, sip up nutrients, and bask in the sun. They inhale nitrogen. They exhale oxygen. Provided they're plunked in the right spot, trees grow automatically. Your spiritual life is supposed to be the same way. When you're connected to God, you get everything you need to wise up and live right. There is, however, one thing that makes you totally different from a tree. You have legs. Trees bloom where they're planted. You have the opportunity to plant yourself where you'll bloom. You have the choice to wander off—or to tap into the things that make you grow.

BRAIN DRAIN What do you think makes it possible for a person to wise up and choose good rather than get sucked into stupidity and choose evil?

FLASHBACK It's not until the New Testament that we hear much about the Holy Spirit. Along with the Father and the Son—Jesus—the Spirit is fully God, the third "person" in our God that the Bible presents as a "Trinity." Jesus promised that when he went back to heaven after walking on earth, the Spirit would come to us as our "Counselor" or "Comforter" (John 14:16). We know that the Spirit teaches us (John 14:26). He gives us gifts to do God's work (1 Corinthians 12, 14). He guides us (Romans 8:1–27). He empowers us to tell others about Christ (Acts 1:8). And in this Bible Chunk, we learn that he turns each of us into an overflowing bowl of fruit.

BIBLE CHUNK Read Galatians 5:16-25

(16) So I say, live by the Spirit, and you will not gratify the desires of the sinful nature. (17) For the sinful nature desires what is contrary to the Spirit, and the Spirit what is contrary to the sinful nature. They are in conflict with each other, so that you do not do what you want. (18) But if you are led by the Spirit, you are not under law.

(19) The acts of the sinful nature are obvious: sexual immorality, impurity and debauchery; (20) idolatry and witchcraft; hatred, discord, jealousy, fits of rage, selfish ambition, dissensions, factions (21) and envy; drunkenness, orgies, and the like. I warn you, as I did before, that those who live like this will not inherit the kingdom of God.

(22) But the fruit of the Spirit is love, joy, peace, patience, kindness, goodness, faithfulness, (23) gentleness and self-control. Against such things there is no law. (24) Those who belong to Christ Jesus have crucified the sinful nature with its passions and desires. (25) Since we live by the Spirit, let us keep in step with the Spirit. (26) Let us not become conceited, provoking and envying each other.

STUFF TO KNOW If you "live by the Spirit," what won't happen (verse 16)?

What two things are fighting inside you (verse 17)?

INSIGHT The "sinful nature" this Bible Chunk talks about is what each of us looks like apart from God enabling us to wise up and live like God wants. The point isn't that any of us is guilty of all of the sins Paul lists next—well, probably not. But those are the sorts of things that naturally gush out of us. The fruit of the Spirit, on the other hand, are the things the Spirit produces when we let him work on us.

What sort of stuff do we see when our "sinful nature" rules (verses 19-21)?

DA'SCOOP Here's what some of those big unfamiliar words in 19–21 mean: "sexual immorality" (any type of sexual relationship outside of marriage); "impurity" (moral uncleanness); "debauchery" (open disregard for what's right); "idolatry" (worshiping anything other than God); "witchcraft" (toying with or worshiping evil powers); "dissensions" and "factions" (divisions and feuding); "drunkenness" and "orgies" (both refer to flagrant abuse of alcohol). Notice Paul wraps up with "and the like," meaning that the sinful nature can whip up lots of other kinds of evil as well.

INSIGHT When Paul says that "those who live like this will not inherit the kingdom of God" (verse 21), he isn't talking about Christians who stumble occasionally. The grammar indicates a *habit* of giving in to sin. People who do those things show they haven't received God's Spirit.

If that's the ugliness we manage all on our own, what fruit does the Holy Spirit grow in us (verses 22–23)?

INSIGHT Verse 24 says that when you wised up and came to Christ, you turned your back on sin—that evil you wanted to do and sometimes did. This ditching sin is what the Bible calls "repentance." It's a decision you make and keep making.

BIG QUESTIONS When God's Spirit and your sinful nature battle inside you, who usually wins?

How big is the battle between right and wrong you feel going on inside you? Pick one: (a) all quiet on the ugly front, (b) guns and grenades, (c) tanks and fighter planes, or (d) atomic bombs by the billions.

How do you see the Spirit growing good fruit in your life?

Can you think of ways you're caving in to the wrong side on the war within? What can you do to be planted in the right spot—so that the Spirit can work in you, growing what grows naturally in a Christian?

SIDELIGHT A few verses after this Bible Chunk, Paul says that when you say yes to the Spirit and obey God, you stay in the right spot for God to grow you some more. When you give in to your sinful nature, you shrivel and die. He put it like this:

> Don't be misled. Remember that you can't ignore God and get away with it. You will always reap what you sow! Those who live only to satisfy their own sinful desires will harvest the consequences of decay and death. But those who live to please the Spirit will harvest everlasting life from the Spirit. So don't get tired of doing what is good. Don't get discouraged and give up, for we will reap a harvest of blessing at the appropriate time. (Galatians 6:7–9 NLT)

DEEP THOT Jesus killed the power of your sin by dying on the cross and giving you a fresh start of forgiveness and a new friendship with him. When you give in to sin, you let the sinful nature climb out of the grave. It will climb all over you.

STICKY STUFF Remind yourself of all that the Spirit is aiming to do inside you by memorizing Galatians 5:22–23.

ACT ON IT Make a list of all the people, hobbies, interests, and hangouts that occupy your day. Which grow good fruit?

DIG ON Slide over to Romans 8:1–17 to hear more about the work of the Spirit inside you.

2. Oops! I Did It Again
Getting up and growing on

Becka pushed her head into her pillow and bawled. She was way beyond furious at herself, at the situation, at the pain she'd caused. She was supposed to be watching her two-year-old brother while her mom ran errands. She was yakking on the phone with a friend—something her mom had told her over and over never to do when she was baby-sitting. Jordan toddled into the backyard and scooted up a neighbor's big, wooden jungle gym—and fell. Now Jordan had a bloody gash on his forehead. Becka had a bottomless pit in her stomach.

BRAIN DRAIN How do you get up and go on when you've done something wrong?

FLASHBACK Right before this Bible Chunk, Paul listed all the reasons he had to be proud—his heritage, education, and ultra-religious accomplishments. Yet in this passage, he shatters them all, arguing that they are worthless compared to one thing: knowing Jesus. What's amazing is how Paul—the guy who wrote a large Chunk of the Bible—still thinks he has plenty of room to grow spiritually. Even Paul has to deal with failures.

BIBLE CHUNK Read Philippians 3:7–14

(7) But whatever was to my profit I now consider loss for the sake of Christ. (8) What is more, I consider everything a loss compared to the surpassing greatness of knowing Christ Jesus my Lord, for whose sake I have lost all things. I consider them rubbish, that I may gain Christ (9) and be

found in him, not having a righteousness of my own that comes from the law, but that which is through faith in Christ—the righteousness that comes from God and is by faith. (10) I want to know Christ and the power of his resurrection and the fellowship of sharing in his sufferings, becoming like him in his death, (11) and so, somehow, to attain to the resurrection from the dead.

(12) Not that I have already obtained all this, or have already been made perfect, but I press on to take hold of that for which Christ Jesus took hold of me. (13) Brothers, I do not consider myself yet to have taken hold of it. But one thing I do: Forgetting what is behind and straining toward what is ahead, (14) I press on toward the goal to win the prize for which God has called me heavenward in Christ Jesus.

STUFF TO KNOW What does Paul think is way better than the things he used to cherish (verses 7–8)?

DA'SCOOP When Paul says that these things are "rubbish," he's not just spewing holy talk. What he actually said was that compared to knowing Christ, all the things he thought were important were "worthless trash," or to be more vivid, "dung" (KJV).

What brand of "righteousness"—good standing with God—was Paul looking for? What kind didn't he want (verse 9)?

INSIGHT You get a picture of Paul, don't you? He's an intense follower of Jesus. Wouldn't you think that someone like him—someone at the peak of the pile of spiritually mature people—would figure some of his accomplishments were worth parading in front of God? But for all his achievements, Paul still knew that he could be friends with God only because Christ had died on the cross for the sins of humankind. He still had to find a way through his failures.

How does Paul talk about the depth of his relationship with Christ—the friendship for which Christ took hold of him? Is it totally complete (verses 12–13)?

When Paul realizes his relationship with God isn't yet perfect, how does he press on? And what does he see on the other side of the finish line (verses 13–14)?

BIG QUESTIONS Maybe you never mess up. Maybe you've never sinned since the day you decided to follow Jesus. But suppose you did. How would you put your friendship with God back together?

What if your failures happened more than once? What would keep you from getting frustrated and giving up?

When Paul blew it—when he got proud of his pre-Christian past, or he rubbed his gargantuan accomplishments as a Christian in someone's face, or he just plain sinned in some other way—how do you think he reacted? What does verse 13 tell you he did?

SIDELIGHT If we're honest, we all have reasons to bury our face in a pillow and bawl. We've all done things we're not proud of—unkind things we've said, ugly things we've done. First John 1:8 puts it bluntly: "If we say we have no sin, we are only fooling ourselves and refusing to accept the truth" (NLT).

When you act in a way that's less than wise—when you do

wrong toward God and other people—you could act like it's no big deal. But it is. If you brush it off, you're searing your conscience so you won't feel guilty again—which is about as wise as killing nerves by plopping your hand on a hot grill. But there's another way to deal with sin: Admit it and get rid of it God's way. First John 1:9 says this: "But if we confess our sins to him, he is faithful and just to forgive us and to cleanse us from every wrong" (NLT).

Part of meaning you're truly sorry for sin is doing your best to fix what you broke. But how do you do this other part—daily owning up to your sins before God?

DEEP THOT Confessing your sins and accepting God's forgiveness is God's way of getting up and going on. Paul aimed to do this: Forget what's behind and strain toward what's ahead. Real Christians aren't people who never fall down; they're the ones who get up and keep going.

STICKY STUFF Get Philippians 3:13–14 in your head and you'll be able to get up and go on.

ACT ON IT Ever have guilt cling to you like the smell of a skunk? Make a list of the things you feel bad about. Tell God you're sorry about those things once and for all—and want nothing more to do with the wrong you did—and ask him to help you get up and go on. Then crumple up your list and toss it in the trash. Wave *buh-bye* to those sins when the garbage truck comes, because that's how God sees it: "As far as the east is from the west, so far has he removed our transgressions from us" (Psalm 103:12).

DIG ON Dig in to 1 John 1:5–2:6 for a boost back up when you fall down.

10. Scrambling Up the Steep Side
God won't ever stop working in you

"I hate you!" Jeff screamed. "I can't do this!" Jeff hung by his finger-tips and his toes halfway up a side of a biggish outcrop, which was halfway up a monstrously biggish cliff. Jeff's older brother, Eric, had a gift for towing Jeff into unexpected adventures—as in I-think-I'm-going-to-die adventures. Jeff tried to calm himself. *Yeah, the view from the top will be cool.* And then he screamed again.

"You can't do this *by yourself*, you mean," Eric said matter-of-factly from a few feet away. "I'm here. Next to your left hip there's a place for your foot—and a foot above your right hand there's a handhold. You know, I wouldn't have brought you up here if you weren't ready for it."

BRAIN DRAIN When wising up and standing clear of sin's unsmartness feels like an impossibly scary climb, what keeps you moving upward?

FLASHBACK The Christians at Philippi had become some of the apostle Paul's biggest friends. When he was imprisoned for his faith at Rome, they had sent money (Philippians 1:5; 4:10–19). Unlike others who were embarrassed when Paul was arrested, the Philippians stood rock-solid with him. Like him, they battled people who opposed their faith (1:29–30).

BIBLE CHUNK Read Philippians 1:3–11

(3) I thank my God every time I remember you. (4) In all my prayers for all of you, I always pray with joy (5) because of your partnership in the

gospel from the first day until now, (6) being confident of this, that he who began a good work in you will carry it on to completion until the day of Christ Jesus.

(7) It is right for me to feel this way about all of you, since I have you in my heart; for whether I am in chains or defending and confirming the gospel, all of you share in God's grace with me. (8) God can testify how I long for all of you with the affection of Christ Jesus.

(9) And this is my prayer: that your love may abound more and more in knowledge and depth of insight, (10) so that you may be able to discern what is best and may be pure and blameless until the day of Christ, (11) filled with the fruit of righteousness that comes through Jesus Christ—to the glory and praise of God.

STUFF TO KNOW Paul sounds a tad excited to have the Philippians as friends. Why (verse 5)?

What was Paul sure that God would totally accomplish in the Philippians (verse 6)?

And exactly how long would God keep working in the folks at Philippi (verse 6)?

Is Paul just being sappy, or does he have a solid reason for being so glad? What is it (verse 7)?

INSIGHT When Paul looked at the Philippians, the evidence that God had started to work in their lives and that their relationships with God were real smacked him in the face. But even though Paul really liked the Philippians, he wasn't thinking only of *their own efforts* when he said they would keep on growing. He promised that *God was working in them*—and would keep up his work until it was finished on the "day of Jesus Christ."

SIDELIGHT By the way, the "day of Jesus Christ" is the time in the future when Jesus returns to earth. It's when evildoers will be judged. But it's also when Christians meet Jesus face-to-face and will be fully changed to be like him. You can learn more at 1 Corinthians 1:8 and 5:5, and at 1 Thessalonians 5:2.

Having seen all this—the Philippians' tenacity and God's radical work in them—what does Paul pray? How can the Philippians expect to grow (verses 9–11)? Finish up Paul's prayers:

- He wants them to have love that abounds in . . .

- And knowledge that helps them . . .

- So they can be . . .

- And be filled with . . .

BIG QUESTIONS How would you like your relationship with God to grow in the next five years?

When you think about wising up and getting to know God better, what part feels like you're hanging to a cliff by your fingernails—feels so difficult it makes you want to shake?

If you could pick one attitude you have that you wish God would rearrange so you'd think more like him, what would it be?

If you could name one action or bad behavior you would like God to help you ditch, what would it be?

What can you do to help those things happen?

How can you count on God to help you grow?

DEEP THOT The path of spiritual growth can feel like climbing a cliff. But ultimately it's God's job to get you to the top. You supply the willingness. He puts in the power and picks the route. Your real confidence is in him.

STICKY STUFF Remember God's promise in Philippians 1:6. If you've started on a real friendship with God, it's a promise for you.

ACT ON IT Pick out a friend who wants to wise up and grow close to God. Pray Paul's prayer for a friend. Pray it for yourself. And ask a friend to pray that prayer for wild growth for you.

DIG ON Flip in your Bible to Ephesians 3:14–21 for another one of Paul's prayers for growth.

Talk About It • 2

EMPATHIZE: What's going on in your life?
ENCOURAGE: How are you doing with Jesus?
EQUIP: What one truth will you take home today?

- What do you do when you want to get rid of evil in your life—like breaking a bad habit or quitting something you know is wrong? (Study 6)
- What's it mean to "first clean the inside of the cup"? (Study 6)
- What has God's power done for you? What do his promises help you do? (Study 7)
- What do you think makes it possible for people to wise up and choose good rather than get sucked into stupidity and choose evil? (Study 8)
- How does the Holy Spirit help you change? (Study 8)
- How do you get up and go on when you've done something wrong? (Study 9)
- What was Paul's secret to pressing on? (Study 9)
- What does 1 John 1:9 say? (Study 9)
- How would you like your relationship with God to grow in the next five years? (Study 10)
- How long will God keep helping you grow? Why would you want that? (Study 10)

SCRUBBING UP YOUR ATTITUDES

11. Say No to Stupidity
God's grace teaches you to say "No!"

Between your feet—and a hundred feet below—you see a rush of white, a foaming river twisting through a rocky canyon. You've never been on a see-through bridge before, but standing on rotted old planks and peering through gaping holes, you can see plenty. "It's okay," your friend calls from ahead. "I've been over it a dozen times." You hesitate. A hundred yards downriver is another bridge—brand-new, built of concrete strong enough for a line of loaded tractor trailers. You want to go with your friend. But you hesitate. You might get away with it once. Or twice. Or a dozen times. But sooner or later you'll have a gut-splattering landing on the rocks below.

BRAIN DRAIN What's the most *dangerous* thing you've ever done?

FLASHBACK You've figured out that God wants you to wise up. And he's remaking you from the inside out. Well, the huge changes he wants to do in you fall into two handy categories. He wants to *rearrange your attitudes*. And he wants to *alter your actions*. In the next five studies you'll redecorate your brain with five new 'tudes. God wants you to *be sure, be yourself, be humble, be stuck on him,* and *be fearless*.

Just before this first Bible Chunk, Paul wrote to his friend Titus with wise instructions for specific groups, including young women and men. (Remember those cavemen-like Cretans?) And then he says this:

BIBLE CHUNK Read Titus 2:11–15

(11) For the grace of God that brings salvation has appeared to all men. (12) It teaches us to say "No" to ungodliness and worldly passions, and to live self-controlled, upright and godly lives in this present age, (13) while we wait for the blessed hope—the glorious appearing of our great God and Savior, Jesus Christ, (14) who gave himself for us to redeem us from all wickedness and to purify for himself a people that are his very own, eager to do what is good.

(15) These, then, are the things you should teach. Encourage and rebuke with all authority. Do not let anyone despise you.

STUFF TO KNOW What does God's grace teach you to say "no" to (verse 12)?

DA'SCOOP "Ungodliness" is the bad attitude that God doesn't matter in life—and all the evil actions that result when you ignore God and his commands. "Worldly passions" are cravings to do what's wrong.

What kind of life does God's grace teach you to say "Yes" to (verse 12)?

DA'SCOOP "Grace" is a huge idea in Scripture. A quick definition: Grace is God's "unmerited favor" toward you. It's the motive behind all of God's forgiveness, friendship, and fatherliness. And "salvation" is the name for this package of all God does to rescue you from sin and build a relationship with you.

What are Christians waiting for (verse 13)? Why does that matter?

Why does God want to "redeem" you from "all wickedness," to yank you out of doing evil and help you decide to do good (verse 14)?

BIG QUESTIONS Suppose you could be bad all you wanted and never get caught. Would that be a good thing?

Does doing evil have consequences beyond getting caught and getting punished? Always? Immediately?

How would you feel if you were Titus and God told you these "are the things you should teach" (verse 15)? How would you explain to your friends that you think it's worth it to say "No" to ungodliness?

INSIGHT Saying "No" to unwise stuff isn't about avoiding all risks or always playing life safe. Following God can be both daring and dangerous. It's about picking the path that's smart, the one you know will support you. It's ditching sin and doing what's right. It's a basic choice: Do you think God's wisdom is truly wise—or way less than half-witted?

So is God smart or stupid?

SIDELIGHT One of the biggest attitudes God wants to

build in you is this: He wants you to *be sure* through and through about your decision to wise up and follow him. Romans 12:1–2 puts it like this:

> (1) Therefore, I urge you, brothers, in view of God's mercy, to offer your bodies as living sacrifices, holy and pleasing to God—this is your spiritual act of worship. (2) Do not conform any longer to the pattern of this world, but be transformed by the renewing of your mind. Then you will be able to test and approve what God's will is—his good, pleasing and perfect will.

Here's what that Bible Chunk feels like in real life: You look at God's goodness to you and think, *Hmmm . . . God is incredibly kind. And mind-bogglingly smart. He sent his Son to die for me. And what he wants for me—his will—is the best life I could imagine. Yep, I think I can trust myself to him. I want to always choose what's wise. To stand clear of sin. To stick close to him.*

That's why you can say "No" to ungodliness. And how you can be sure you want to obey Jesus in every area of life.

DEEP THOT The sureness of your decision to hang on to God's wisdom and walk God's way comes from recognizing God's goodness to you—the undeserved favor he showed you in Christ and the perfection of the paths he picks for you. It's an attitude of gratitude that gladly submits to his will, making choices that don't send you splattering.

STICKY STUFF Stick Titus 2:11–12 in your brain juice and you'll stay safe in God's love.

ACT ON IT Ask a Christian who's a few years older than you how they grew sure they wanted to follow God.

DIG ON Read Joshua 24:14–15, where Joshua told a crowd of people he was without-a-doubt sure he wanted to follow God.

12. You Get a Standing "O"
There's nothing better than being you

Nina cringed as the conversation at her lunch table rambled off without her—*blah, blah, bla-bla-blah*. Okay, so nobody was interested in how her solo at the violin recital went. Truth is, she made that fiddle smoke and she got a howling standing "O" from the 3 teachers, 26 students, and 203 other people there. It mattered to her, but she wished it mattered to her friends.

BRAIN DRAIN What's the best thing about you that's different from most other people?

FLASHBACK This Bible Chunk is plunked into the middle of a passage on spiritual gifts—special gifts God's Spirit puts in us to build God's kingdom. But what it says applies to your whole life.

BIBLE CHUNK Read 1 Corinthians 12:14–26

(14) Now the body is not made up of one part but of many. (15) If the foot should say, "Because I am not a hand, I do not belong to the body," it would not for that reason cease to be part of the body. (16) And if the ear should say, "Because I am not an eye, I do not belong to the body," it would not for that reason cease to be part of the body. (17) If the whole body were an eye, where would the sense of hearing be? If the whole body were an ear, where would the sense of smell be? (18) But in fact God has arranged the parts in the body, every one of them, just as he wanted them to be. (19) If they were all one part, where would the body be? (20) As it is, there are many parts, but one body.

(21) The eye cannot say to the hand, "I don't need you!" And the head cannot say to the feet, "I don't need you!" (22) On the contrary, those parts of the body that seem to be weaker are indispensable, (23) and the parts

that we think are less honorable we treat with special honor. And the parts that are unpresentable are treated with special modesty, (24) while our presentable parts need no special treatment. But God has combined the members of the body and has given greater honor to the parts that lacked it, (25) so that there should be no division in the body, but that its parts should have equal concern for each other. (26) If one part suffers, every part suffers with it; if one part is honored, every part rejoices with it.

STUFF TO KNOW Use your imagination here: Can a body part up and decide not to be part of the body? Why not (verses 14–17)?

Are all the parts of a body the same? Why not (verses 14–20)?

Who put the parts of the body in place and gave them their jobs (verse 18)?

Can one body part decide another body part isn't necessary—and lop it off? Why not (verses 21–24)?

Do any body parts get special treatment (verses 22–24)?

INSIGHT Big truth: The parts of the body that seem weak or weird are just as indispensable as the buff and beautiful. Paul delicately points out that the body parts that are covered up—your organs and your innards—are worthy of special respect. People everyone would like to ignore evidently are the ones who can fulfill a need in your life no one else can.

What happens if one body part is hurting? What goes on when one body part succeeds (verse 26)?

BIG QUESTIONS When do you battle being your-self? What situations do you face where showing people who you really are will get you mocked?

What things in particular do you hide about you?

If you could share one hidden thing about yourself with one person you could trust, what would it be?

Go back and look at your answers to the three nagging "Why not?" questions on the previous page. See how they all kind of have the same answers? *We need each other. We were made to work together. We can't survive alone. One body part isn't any better than any other.* What does all this say about how we treat people we regard as rejects?

How are you going to react next time someone rejects *you?*

SIDELIGHT You can't force people to value you highly. You can control how you treat others. And you can always decide to be sure in yourself because God made you uniquely *you*. Psalm 139:13–16 says you are "fearfully and wonderfully made." That word "fearfully" sounds like what you maybe look like when you wake up and your hair is all winged out. But what it actually means is "awesomely" or "awe-strikingly." Psalm 139 goes on to say that God's handiwork is unquestionably wonderful, and that God knew exactly what he was doing when you were being assembled in your mother's womb. He even saw your whole life ahead of time . . . but that's an amazing factoid too deep to get into here.

DEEP THOT These are the facts of life, facts so indisputable they're laughable. No eyeball flings itself from its socket. No toe defects from the foot. Just as parts of the body need one another, people—especially in the church—need one another. You and the people around you are each absolutely indispensable and irreversibly connected. Be yourself. The rest can't survive without you.

STICKY STUFF Knock Psalm 139:14 into your noggin until you're convinced that it's true: "I praise you because I am fearfully and wonderfully made; your works are wonderful, I know that full well."

ACT ON IT Ask your youth pastor or volunteer youth leader how today's Bible Chunk (1 Corinthians 12:14–26) does or doesn't describe how the youth at your church get along. And ask what you can do to help.

DIG ON Take a dive into Ephesians 4:7–16, which says that when we don't get along as a body, we're like infants bobbing on an ocean. *Scary.*

(13.) Please Don't Call Him Professor

Hanging on to Christ's humility

As soon as Mrs. Wagner introduced the new kid to her Sunday school class and had each person say his or her name, she announced that they'd all wear name tags for the next few weeks. *Groans.* "You won't need those," the new kid smirked. "I bet I already know everybody's name." That said, he perfectly repeated the names of twenty-six people he'd only just met. "Back at my old school everyone called me 'Professor' because I was so much smarter than them," he gloated. "You can call me that too."

BRAIN DRAIN How do you get along with people who act like snots about their brains, beauty, or bulging muscles?

FLASHBACK Paul's good friends in Philippi were growing—but they weren't perfect. Paul, for example, coached Euodia and Syntyche—two women in the congregation with really tough-to-pronounce names—to get along (Philippians 4:2–3). Paul skimped on the juicy details of their fight, but their problem apparently was obnoxious and well-known enough to raise in a letter meant to be read aloud to every church in the region. The humble attitude he urges in this Bible Chunk is part of his prescription to them and to all Christians.

BIBLE CHUNK Read Philippians 2:1–8

(1) If you have any encouragement from being united with Christ, if any comfort from his love, if any fellowship with the Spirit, if any tenderness

and compassion, (2) then make my joy complete by being like-minded, having the same love, being one in spirit and purpose. (3) Do nothing out of selfish ambition or vain conceit, but in humility consider others better than yourselves. (4) Each of you should look not only to your own inter-ests, but also to the interests of others.
(5) Your attitude should be the same as that of Christ Jesus:
(6) Who, being in very nature God,
    did not consider equality with God something to be grasped,
(7) but made himself nothing,
taking the very nature of a servant,
    being made in human likeness.
(8) And being found in appearance as a man,
    he humbled himself
    and became obedient to death—
    even death on a cross!

STUFF TO KNOW Paul starts off with four "ifs," but by the grammar we know he means "of course these things are true, sooo . . ." What four things do we get—from Christ, his Spirit, and each other (verse 1)?

Since those things are true, what sorts of attitudes and actions can Christians splash on each other (verses 2–4)?

You don't have to wonder what humility looks like. Whose attitude are you supposed to mimic (verse 5)?

Jesus was God. King of the Universe. Ruler of All. How does some-one of that huge stature usually demand to be treated (verse 6)?

INSIGHT Take a gander at this same Bible Chunk in the New Living Translation. It helps you get the coolness of what Jesus did

in clearer language: "Your attitude should be the same that Christ Jesus had. Though he was God, he did not demand and cling to his rights as God. He made himself nothing; he took the humble position of a slave and appeared in human form. And in human form he obediently humbled himself even further by dying a criminal's death on a cross" (Philippians 2:5–8).

Jesus didn't stomp, demand his way, and cause nausea to ooze up from deep inside us by telling us how great he was. What did he do instead? List at least four things (verses 5–8)?

SIDELIGHT
The Bible Chunk you've been reading captures the true humility of Jesus, who on the cross endured the most ugly kind of execution humans ever invented—and all for our sake. The next few verses in Philippians describe how Jesus' one-of-a-kind, incomparable greatness will one day be on display for everyone to see: "God exalted [Jesus]" that at his name "every knee should bow. . . and every tongue confess that Jesus Christ is Lord" (Philippians 2:9–11).

BIG QUESTIONS
If you were incredibly famous, how would you act?

Would you be humble? What does "humility" look like?

If you were God, how would you act? Would you let yourself be nailed naked to a cross for other people's sins?

INSIGHT
Most people think of humility as making yourself

SCRUBBING UP YOUR ATTITUDES

a doormat—lying down so people can step on your back and wipe their shoes on your shirt. Jesus really did take a lowly place, but he did it by choice. And he did it strategically, to reach a goal. When you have his attitude of humility, you act in ways that show others honor (that's the best way to understand verse 3; check out Romans 12:10 too). You no longer think *only* of yourself, but you consider what other people need *as well* (verse 4).

What's the hardest thing for you to swallow about being humble?

What would make it possible for you to act like Jesus did—not to die on the cross, but to have his attitude of humility and "look not only to your own interests, but also to the interests of others"? Hint: What do verses 1–2 say?

DEEP THOT The cross was Jesus' ultimate display of humility—and the perfect example of the attitude God wants to plant in you. Jesus once described the outcome of humility this way: "For whoever exalts himself will be humbled, and whoever humbles himself will be exalted" (Matthew 23:12). His life, death, and resurrection proves he knew what he was talking about.

STICKY STUFF You'll be really smart if you remember Philippians 2:4–5.

ACT ON IT Do one thing today that shows honor to another person by putting his or her interests before yours.

DIG ON Read John 13:1–17 for a vivid illustration of Jesus' humility.

14. Stuffed With Stuff
Get filled up with God

Balloons! You stare at your mom's idea of a suave sweater vest—
one she picked for you to wear to a school concert. Yeah, it was
really hip—back in 1957. How could she expect you to wear that
thing? What does she think your friends are going to say when they
see those hot air balloon thingies sewn across the front? Does she
want to dress you up like a dork?

BRAIN DRAIN What kind of stuff do you need to feel
like you fit in with your peers?

FLASHBACK You've seen the five Cs of being cool at
school: Clothes, CDs, Computers, Cash, and—when you hit high
school—Cars. It's true that Jesus never even owned three out of
those five items, but he still had a wise thing or two to say about
things. He didn't say that stuff was necessarily bad. He just made it
clear it wasn't the best.

BIBLE CHUNK Read Matthew 6:19-34

(19) "Do not store up for yourselves treasures on earth, where moth
and rust destroy, and where thieves break in and steal. (20) But store up
for yourselves treasures in heaven, where moth and rust do not destroy,
and where thieves do not break in and steal. (21) For where your treasure
is, there your heart will be also.

(22) "The eye is the lamp of the body. If your eyes are good, your whole
body will be full of light. (23) But if your eyes are bad, your whole body
will be full of darkness. If then the light within you is darkness, how great
is that darkness!

(24) "No one can serve two masters. Either he will hate the one and love the other, or he will be devoted to the one and despise the other. You cannot serve both God and Money.

(25) "Therefore I tell you, do not worry about your life, what you will eat or drink; or about your body, what you will wear. Is not life more important than food, and the body more important than clothes? (26) Look at the birds of the air; they do not sow or reap or store away in barns, and yet your heavenly Father feeds them. Are you not much more valuable than they? (27) Who of you by worrying can add a single hour to his life?

(28) And why do you worry about clothes? See how the lilies of the field grow. They do not labor or spin. (29) Yet I tell you that not even Solomon in all his splendor was dressed like one of these. (30) If that is how God clothes the grass of the field, which is here today and tomorrow is thrown into the fire, will he not much more clothe you, O you of little faith? (31) So do not worry, saying, 'What shall we eat?' or 'What shall we drink?' or 'What shall we wear?' (32) For the pagans run after all these things, and your heavenly Father knows that you need them. (33) But seek first his kingdom and his righteousness, and all these things will be given to you as well. (34) Therefore do not worry about tomorrow, for tomorrow will worry about itself. Each day has enough trouble of its own."

STUFF TO KNOW What happens to stuff you cling to on earth? What happens to stuff you stash up in heaven (verses 19–20)?

How do you suppose it's possible to have treasure in heaven? What does it have to do with your heart (verses 20–21)?

What do you think Jesus meant when he said you "cannot serve both God and money" (verse 24)?

SIDELIGHT You've no doubt heard people babble that "money is the root of all evil" as if they pulled that saying straight out of the Bible. What Scripture actually says is that "the *love* of money is the root of *all kinds of* evil" (1 Timothy 6:10, italics added).

That same Bible Chunk also explains why we can't fall in love with cold hard cash and all the things it can buy: "People who want to get rich fall into temptation and a trap and into many foolish and harmful desires that plunge men into ruin and destruction" (1 Timothy 6:9). "Ruin and destruction" sounds, um . . . *serious*.

So if everything on earth sooner or later rots or rusts, what kind of attitude can you have toward your life? What shouldn't you worry endlessly about (verses 25–31)?

Is Jesus nuts? How can you have that kind of attitude (verses 26, 30, 32)?

BIG QUESTIONS What's one thing you're dying to own that you don't?

Knowing what you know from Matthew 6, do you think God wants you to have that thingy—or two or three? Why or why not?

What test did Jesus give in the first half of Matthew 6:33—the test of whether you're too wrapped up in your stuff?

SIDELIGHT Big Bible example: God made gold, and gold is a good thing. But back in the Old Testament, God's people melted their jewelry, cast a statue of a baby cow, and all bowed down in worship. They made a good thing bad (Exodus 32:15–35).

That's a wildly goofy scene only until you ponder the fact that people still do the same thing. If you let something get bigger than God—and his "kingdom," his reign and purposes in your life—then you've made an "idol" just like that golden calf.

Maybe you remember when God gave Moses the Ten Commandments etched on two stone tablets. Well, the sin of turning gold into a god was so serious that when Moses found out about it he smashed the tablets onto the ground in anger. And do you know what commandment was carved at the very top of those tablets? "I am the Lord your God, who brought you out of Egypt, out of the land of slavery. *You shall have no other gods before me*" (Exodus 20:2-3, italics added). Now, that's the stuff at the top of God's got-to-have-it list.

What does Jesus promise you in the second half of Matthew 6:33—provided you pass the test in the first half?

DEEP THOT More than anything else, God wants you filled up on him, not stuffed with stuff. If you're not stuck on God, you're stuck in some seriously unholy mud.

STICKY STUFF You won't get mixed up about what's most important if you mix Matthew 6:33 into your brain matter.

ACT ON IT Take some time today to scan your stuff. Has any of it become more important to you than God? How do you know he's at the top of your list of what you want out of life?

DIG ON Check out Exodus 32:1-35 to get the whole story of how God's people made gold into a god. Notice this: The Israelites melted their gold and made the golden calf the minute they stopped believing that God cared for them.

15. Holy Boldness
Owning up to the One who owns you

Being bold as a Christian doesn't mean you have to stand up and yodel a prayer for your lunch. It doesn't always mean you debate every teacher who doesn't believe in God. It probably doesn't mean a gunman will rampage through your school and hurt you because you believe in Jesus. It does mean, however, that you own up to your friendship with the One who owns you.

BRAIN DRAIN Suppose your peers decided they didn't like you—or your faith. What's the absolutely nastiest, most gargantuanly terrible thing they could do to you?

FLASHBACK Jesus spoke the words in this Bible Chunk as he sent out his twelve closest followers to teach that "the kingdom of heaven is near" (Matthew 10:7). He warned these newbie preachers that some people would accept them—but that others would smoke them. They might be handed over to councils and beaten, but even as they stood before kings and governors God would give them the right words to speak (Matthew 10:19–20). So the people at the beginning of this Bible Chunk Jesus referred to as "those who kill the body" are a whole range of folks out to rough up followers of Jesus. Even in the face of these deadly persecutors the disciples could be fearless. Here's why:

BIBLE CHUNK Read Matthew 10:28–33

(28) "Do not be afraid of those who kill the body but cannot kill the soul. Rather, be afraid of the One who can destroy both soul and body in

hell. (29) Are not two sparrows sold for a penny? Yet not one of them will fall to the ground apart from the will of your Father. (30) And even the very hairs of your head are all numbered. (31) So don't be afraid; you are worth more than many sparrows.

(32) Whoever acknowledges me before men, I will also acknowledge him before my Father in heaven. (33) But whoever disowns me before men, I will disown him before my Father in heaven."

STUFF TO KNOW Jesus is talking about some blunt stuff. What's the absolute worst that people who don't like believers can do (verse 28)?

That's all they can do? What a relief, huh? Not really? But if that's bad, what can God do to those who reject him (verse 28)?

SIDELIGHT The Bible says that "whoever rejects the Son will not see life, for God's wrath remains on him" (John 3:36), and that "It is a dreadful thing to fall into the hands of the living God" (Hebrews 10:31). That's scary stuff. But if you're a Christian, you don't have to fear God's judgment. Here's why: "At one time you were separated from God. You were his enemies in your minds, and the evil things you did were against God. But now God has made you his friends again. He did this through Christ's death in the body so that he might bring you into God's presence as people who are holy, with no wrong, and with nothing of which God can judge you guilty" (Colossians 1:21–22 NCV).

What kind of care does God extend to those who belong to him (verses 29–31)?

What evidence does Jesus offer of the kind of care God provides (verses 29–30)?

INSIGHT What's up with that hair-numbering stuff? You might wonder if God has nothing better to do with his time, like you counting bricks in the wall during a boring class. What it means, though, is that God's care for you isn't only about life-or-death issues. The smallest details about you matter to him.

What does Jesus promise to people who willingly admit that they know him (verse 32)?

BIG QUESTIONS How do people treat you when they find out you're a Christian?

When do you get queasy telling others that you are a Christian? When do you clam up?

When have you been able to be bold about what you believe as a Christian? What made it work?

If you could get your peers to understand one fact about what it means to you to be a Christian, what would it be?

INSIGHT Being ashamed of your relationship with God isn't part of his plan for you. If you consistently deny that you know Jesus, then maybe you don't! In fact, part of truly following Jesus is speaking truthfully about your belief in him. Romans 10:9 says that "if you confess with your mouth, 'Jesus is Lord,' and believe in your heart that God raised him from the dead, you will be saved."

But knowing exactly how and when to best speak up doesn't come automatically, and one wise Christian has said that what a public "confession of faith" looks like "will vary in boldness, fluency, wisdom, sensitivity, and frequency from believer to believer." You often learn only through trial and error what it means to be bold without being brash or bossy.

What do you think is a bold and beneficial way you could tell people about the Jesus you know?

DEEP THOT Being up front about your belief in Jesus can be several notches beyond scary. But Proverbs 29:25 (NCV) says "Being afraid of people can get you into trouble, but if you trust the Lord, you will be safe." God told his early disciples and Christians of all times that when they are put to the test, the right words will be on their tongues. Trust that. God wants to get rid of your fear.

STICKY STUFF You can be fearless with Matthew 10:32 on your mind.

ACT ON IT To learn more about persecuted Christians worldwide—not just back in Bible times but in your world *today*— visit *www.opendoors.com*. There's a load of things you can do to help.

DIG ON Read Hebrews 11:32–38 and 2 Corinthians 6:3–10 for a couple catalogs of the boldness of God's people.

Talk About It • 3

EMPATHIZE: What's going on in your life?
ENCOURAGE: How are you doing with Jesus?
EQUIP: What one truth will you take home today?

- Suppose you could be bad all you wanted and never get caught. Would that be a good thing? (Study 11)
- What does God's grace do for you? (Study 11)
- How sure are you that you want to do what God wants? (Study 11)
- Why do we need each other? (Study 12)
- What's the best thing about you that's different from most other people? (Study 12)
- What does humility look like? (Study 13)
- What's the hardest thing for you to swallow about being humble? (Study 13)
- What would make it possible for you to act like Jesus did—to have his attitude of humility that helps you "look not only to your own interests, but also to the interests of others"? (Study 13)
- What kind of material stuff do you feel like you need to fit in with your peers? (Study 14)
- How would you know if you were too wrapped up in your stuff—and squeezing God out of life? (Study 14)
- Suppose your peers decided they didn't like you—or your faith. What would they do to you? (Study 15)
- What does Jesus promise to people who willingly admit that they know him? (Study 15)
- What's a bold and beneficial way you could tell people about the Jesus you know? (Study 15)

PART 4

SUDSING UP YOUR ACTIONS

16. Parental Rights
Getting along at home

It's true: God wants to rearrange your brain. It's in your heart that behavior starts, and the person you are on the inside is the person you become on the outside. So God wants you to be sure about your decision to follow him, to like the gifts he's given you, to grow in humility, to stay stuck on him, and to ditch fear of your peers. But when you wise up and stand clear of the unsmartness of sin, God doesn't just scrub up your attitudes. He wants to suds up your actions, like how you get along with all the people in your life: your parents, people in charge, your enemies, your friends, and the opposite sex. That's what we'll look at in the next five studies.

BRAIN DRAIN What do you think God has do with your getting along with your parents?

FLASHBACK You might not like hearing the word "child" aimed at you or being told to obey your mom and pop, the topic of this Bible Chunk. Yet consider something cool: In these verses Paul shoots God's commands straight to you. He assumed children and parents would be learning side by side, and that you are adult enough to hear God's instructions yourself. He didn't tell parents, "Go home and tell your kids to shape up." When it comes to your life at home, God has some instructions for you. He also has a few words for your folks. It's wisdom for all on how to get along.

BIBLE CHUNK Read Ephesians 6:1–8

(1) Children, obey your parents in the Lord, for this is right. (2) "Honor your father and mother"—which is the first commandment with a prom-

ise—(3) "that it may go well with you and that you may enjoy long life on the earth."

(4) Fathers, do not exasperate your children; instead, bring them up in the training and instruction of the Lord.

(5) Slaves, obey your earthly masters with respect and fear, and with sincerity of heart, just as you would obey Christ. (6) Obey them not only to win their favor when their eye is on you, but like slaves of Christ, doing the will of God from your heart. (7) Serve wholeheartedly, as if you were serving the Lord, not men, (8) because you know that the Lord will reward everyone for whatever good he does, whether he is slave or free.

STUFF TO KNOW What's the command you bang into right at the beginning of this Bible Chunk (verse 1)?

So what's reason number one to obey (verse 1)?

And what's the promise if you do obey (verses 2–3)?

SIDELIGHT The Bible paints obedience to your parents not just as a good idea but as a duty. Obeying is the *right thing* to do. And Colossians 3:20 explains the extent to which you are to obey: "Children, obey your parents *in everything*, for this pleases the Lord" (italics added). The Bible word for "obey" means being ready to hear and carry out instructions, and the grammar shows that action is to be a habit. One more thing: Obeying "in the Lord" means your parents also answer to God.

So if that's *your* duty, what are *parents* supposed to do—or not (verse 4)?

What job does God give parents (verse 4)?

SIDELIGHT The New Century Version of the Bible words a similar Bible Chunk like this: "Fathers, do not nag your children. If you are too hard to please, they may want to stop trying" (Colossians 3:21). So what do you do if your parents provoke you? The Bible doesn't say exactly, but Paul once gave this advice to Timothy: "Never speak harshly to an older man, but appeal to him respectfully as though he were your own father" (1 Timothy 5:1 NLT). Start by losing the harshness. Then try to let the respect you show make your point appealing.

Back in Bible times slavery wasn't what it was in the United States before the Civil War; slaves had families, and people often sold themselves into slavery—for a time—to get ahead. Even so, if your master was nasty, life was hard. Parents aren't slave drivers, yet they do have hefty control of your life. So what lessons can you learn from Paul's instructions to slaves (verses 5–8)?

- How should you obey?

- When should you obey—only when they're looking?

- Who are you really serving?

- What does God promise to those who do good?

BIG QUESTIONS What do you like about your relationship with your parents?

How do you struggle with your parents?

Where do you suppose your parents struggle with you?

INSIGHT What if your parents aren't Christians—or not exactly upstanding members of the First Church of the Spiritually Mature? You've probably figured out that Paul's instructions assume a Christian family sitting together in a Christian setting. You might wonder if you have an excuse to do whatever you want. But unless your parents are abusive or directly contradict God's commands, your duty to obey still rules. Their authority in your life doesn't depend on their knowing God, but on the fact that God gave them the job of guiding you.

DEEP THOT Growing up isn't a chance to escape the control of your parents and others in authority over your life. It's your chance to follow God for yourself. That might be hard to swallow. But next up we'll see how authority works.

STICKY STUFF Remind yourself of Ephesians 6:1 so your parents won't have to.

ACT ON IT Think about how you can talk with your parents about areas where you struggle to obey them—or where you think you've demonstrated the responsibility that sometimes earns more freedom. If you frequently bang heads with your parents, find a wise older Christian who can help you be honest about your own shortcomings—and help you learn to present your case respectfully.

DIG ON Read Luke 2:41–52 for a glimpse of how Jesus got along with his parents. Look at how he thought for himself and yet managed to obey his parents the way God commands.

(17.) On Good Authority
Submitting to authority

Ricky finally graduated to sitting in the front seat with the passenger-side air bag at about the same time his older brother Eddie got his driver's license. And on Ricky and Eddie's first ride minus a parent sitting in the backseat, it was mere seconds after Eddie muttered something like "Let's see what this baby can do!" and swerved into the fast lane that Ricky and Eddie noticed sirens screaming and lights blazing from behind. . . .

BRAIN DRAIN Who is someone in charge of some part of your life that you have a hard time submitting to?

FLASHBACK The book of Romans contains some of the most profound hunks of theology of any book in the Bible—statements about who God is, how he acts, and how we get along with him. Romans is where Paul wrote ultra-important verses like "For all have sinned and fall short of the glory of God" (Romans 3:23) and "For the wages of sin is death, but the gift of God is eternal life in Christ Jesus our Lord" (6:23). It's the book that says to "offer your bodies as living sacrifices, holy and pleasing to God—this is your spiritual act of worship" (12:1). Romans is big-idea stuff. But by the time chapter 13 rolls around, Paul veers into life's nitty-gritty—like dealing with police officers and principals. Not that Paul specifically names those people, but you'll get the idea.

BIBLE CHUNK Read Romans 13:1–5

(1) Everyone must submit himself to the governing authorities, for there is no authority except that which God has established. The authori-

ties that exist have been established by God. (2) Consequently, he who re-bels against the authority is rebelling against what God has instituted, and those who do so will bring judgment on themselves. (3) For rulers hold no terror for those who do right, but for those who do wrong. Do you want to be free from fear of the one in authority? Then do what is right and he will commend you. (4) For he is God's servant to do you good. But if you do wrong, be afraid, for he does not bear the sword for nothing. He is God's servant, an agent of wrath to bring punishment on the wrongdoer. (5) Therefore, it is necessary to submit to the authorities, not only because of possible punishment but also because of conscience.

STUFF TO KNOW What's an "authority"? What's it mean to "submit yourself" (verse 1)?

Where does authority come from (verse 1)?

Soooo . . . follow this reasoning: If authority comes from God and you rebel against an authority in your life, precisely whom are you rebelling against? Hmm? What's the consequence of that (verse 3)?

DA'SCOOP "Authority" in the Bible can be a thing—the right to exercise control—or a person who has that power over others. Either way, the Bible presents authority as a huge character-istic of God, and people only possess authority when God gives it to them.

What's the upside of authorities? What good are they supposed to do (verse 4)?

Should you fear people in positions of power over you? Why or why not (verses 3–4)?

INSIGHT Just because this Bible Chunk says that authority comes from God doesn't mean the Bible is stupid about the nasty qualities of some human authorities. Religious rulers, after all, plotted to do away with Jesus. Roman government officials stood by and permitted him to suffer unjustly. And Roman soldiers carried out the orders to crucify (Matthew 26:1–5; 27:1–31). When Jesus faced these evil rulers, however, his response was shocking. He prayed, "Father, forgive them, for they do not know what they are doing" (Luke 23:34).

What two reasons are there to submit (verse 5)?

INSIGHT Got those two reasons? You submit to authority because you don't like blaring sirens or the big house. To defy some laws means death—a deterrent that keeps most people in line. But punishment isn't the only reason you submit. Your conscience recognizes the rightness of structures God puts in place: Without leaders containing us we would clobber one another. The only thing worse than living in a world where everyone seems to boss you around would be living in a world where no one does.

BIG QUESTIONS What do you think of the Bible's command to submit to authority?

When have you been rebelling when you should have been submitting?

When do you think it's right *not* to submit to authority? How would you wisely rebel without undercutting God's goals?

SIDELIGHT Daniel wouldn't pray to King Darius—and was fed to lions (Daniel 6). Shadrach, Meshach, and Abednego refused to bow to an idol—and were tossed into a furnace (Daniel 3). Peter kept on preaching when the religious rulers told him to stop—and was thrown in prison again and again (Acts 4:18–22). Each refused to comply with ungodly orders. But by accepting the consequences of their "rebellion," they still upheld the concept of authority. Church history shows that many Christians followed Paul's advice and refused to revolt against their governments even in the face of torture and murder. Paul's words weren't cheap; he himself likely died at the hands of evil authorities.

DEEP THOT Most of us seldom face rulers so evil that disobeying them is our only godly choice. We're way more likely to disobey for the chance to make our own choices.

STICKY STUFF You'll steer straight with Romans 13:1 in your cerebrum.

ACT ON IT Keep track today of any times your skin crawls just because someone in authority over you—parents, bosses, teachers—makes you do something.

DIG ON Read 1 Peter 4:12–19 and 2:13–25 for insights into suffering for doing right.

(18.) Toss Another Brain on the Barby

Dealing with cruel people

Becka twisted to see over her shoulder—and to study her rear in a full-length mirror. She still burned at Renee for calling her "bubble butt" in front of half the school. *I'm so sick of Renee pretending to be my friend*, she screamed inside. *It's time I start treating her like the enemy she is.*

BRAIN DRAIN How do you react when a friend or foe goes cruel all over you? Do you hold back—or hit back?

FLASHBACK In thirty-three years of life on earth, Jesus met up with all the cruelty humankind could muster. He suffered insults, personal attacks, and threats on his life—threats that ultimately came to pass at his crucifixion. Incredibly, he didn't dish back the unkindness: "When they hurled their insults at him, he did not retaliate; when he suffered, he made no threats" (1 Peter 2:23). And just as incredibly, God expects the same behavior from us (1 Peter 2:21). In this Bible Chunk, Paul details for the Romans what Jesus-like actions toward enemies look like.

BIBLE CHUNK Read Romans 12:14–21

(14) Bless those who persecute you; bless and do not curse. (15) Rejoice with those who rejoice; mourn with those who mourn. (16) Live in harmony with one another. Do not be proud, but be willing to associate with people of low position. Do not be conceited.

(17) Do not repay anyone evil for evil. Be careful to do what is right in the eyes of everybody. (18) If it is possible, as far as it depends on you, live at peace with everyone. (19) Do not take revenge, my friends, but leave room for God's wrath, for it is written: "It is mine to avenge; I will repay," says the Lord. (20) On the contrary:
"If your enemy is hungry, feed him;
if he is thirsty, give him something to drink.
In doing this, you will heap burning coals on his head."
(21) Do not be overcome by evil, but overcome evil with good.

STUFF TO KNOW Maybe you remember from the first study in *Wise Up* that "blessed" more or less means "happy." What do you think about bequeathing bundles of joy to your enemies (verse 14)?

SIDELIGHT Paul—the writer of this Bible Chunk—didn't have to invent the idea of being kind to your persecutors. Jesus himself said, "You have heard that it was said, 'Love your neighbor and hate your enemy.' But I tell you: Love your enemies and pray for those who persecute you" (Matthew 5:43–44).

There's a bundle of character traits that go along with the ability to bless bad guys. What are they (verses 15–16)?

Here's where Paul gets specific: Name four things you can do to "bless" the people who make your life miserable (verses 17–19).

• Do not . . .

• Be careful to . . .

• As far as it depends on you . . .

• Do not . . .

Why in the world would you decide to act like that (verse 19)?

Whose responsibility is it to pay back evil? Or put it this way: Who will do the job and do it right (verse 19)?

SIDELIGHT Some people think that "wrath" is what God is all about. It's true that God is holy—totally pure—and that his holiness means he is wholly against sin. Truth is, most people wouldn't want God to be any other way. We wouldn't want to live in a world where evil never gets its due. We want God to do away with evil, pronto. Problem is, we'd like to slap that standard on someone else, but we wouldn't like to live under it ourselves. Fortunately for *all* of us, God's wrath is his last resort. God isn't eager to toast evildoers; he's ready to take us back into a relationship with him. Peter wrote, "He is patient with you, not wanting anyone to perish, but everyone to come to repentance" (2 Peter 3:9). He tells us to let him do his job of judgment because only he—with his perfect knowledge—will pay back evil with perfect fairness.

What happens if you do good to an enemy (verse 20)?

INSIGHT If you pay back evil with kindness, you mess with your enemy's mind. It's like barbecuing your enemy's brain. He or she might feel regretful enough to change—or even astounded enough to make the huge change of believing in and following God.

What's God's best way for you to get even with evil (verse 21)?

BIG QUESTION One kind of enemy is your best friend who goes bad on you once in a while. The other kind is the kid who shows up over and over in your nightmares—except you're not sleeping. How would either of those kinds respond if you acted on the commands in this Bible Chunk?

Do you think that refusing to take revenge means volunteering to be physically or emotionally trounced? Why or why not?

The next time someone trashes you, what will you do?

DEEP THOT The Bible once again isn't stupid. There's no promise in Scripture that every enemy you bless will fall at your feet begging to be your friend. And Jesus offered specific instructions on how to confront evil (Matthew 18:15–17). Yet showing Christ's patience in doing good hikes up the possibility of good coming out of bad. Choosing to bless your enemies feels like a weird way to wise up. But remember: The thing you're doing is trusting God to do his thing.

STICKY STUFF You'll leave room for God's revenge if you burn Romans 12:19 into your brain.

ACT ON IT Pick an enemy and heap burning coals on his or her head with a surprise act of kindness.

DIG ON Read 2 Peter 1:22–25, where you hear how Jesus reacted to people who hated him.

19. The Yoke's on You
Being tight with the right people

Sammi and Kara grew up as next-door neighbors and the best of friends. They still played volleyball and they still rode their bikes around the neighborhood. But with every month that passed it seemed like they had less and less to talk about. And especially after Sammi went on a mission trip the summer after eighth grade, it was like they didn't know each other anymore.

BRAIN DRAIN Who is your closest friend? What makes her or him so near and dear?

FLASHBACK Some of the words in this Bible Chunk aren't ones you use or hook together every day, so it sounds a bit preacherish and superspiritually hyper-religious. But it relays some huge wisdom on what kind of friends to bond with and how to get along with people who don't believe what you do.

BIBLE CHUNK Read 2 Corinthians 6:14–18

(14) Do not be yoked together with unbelievers. For what do righteousness and wickedness have in common? Or what fellowship can light have with darkness? (15) What harmony is there between Christ and Belial? What does a believer have in common with an unbeliever? (16) What agreement is there between the temple of God and idols? For we are the temple of the living God. As God has said: "I will live with them and walk among them, and I will be their God, and they will be my people."

(17) "Therefore come out from them
and be separate,
says the Lord.

Touch no unclean thing,
and I will receive you."
(18) "I will be a Father to you,
and you will be my sons and daughters,
says the Lord Almighty."

STUFF TO KNOW So what exactly are you not supposed to do with a non-Christian? What do you think that means (verse 14)?

Why won't it work for a Christian and non-Christian to be yoked together? What four pairs of things can't get along (verses 14–16)?

DA'SCOOP "Belial" is a name for Satan that means "scoundrel."

INSIGHT A yoke is a hunk of wood that lashes animals together for plowing and pulling. So what this Bible Chunk means is this: "Don't team up with those who are unbelievers" (NLT) or "Do not join yourselves to them" (NCV). The whole purpose of a yoke is to make two big animals go in the same direction. But if you get yoked with someone who doesn't want to pull in God's direction, that's a problem—because pretty soon you're likely to be going the *wrong* direction.

SIDELIGHT Here's the other hard part about getting lashed together with nonbelievers. If you're a Christian, you're already yoked to Jesus. In Matthew 11:28–29 Jesus said, "Come to me, all of you who are weary and carry heavy burdens, and I will give you rest. Take my yoke upon you. Let me teach you, because I am humble and gentle, and you will find rest for your souls. For my yoke fits perfectly, and the burden I give you is light" (NLT). When Jesus is the one leading you where you want to go, you've got one great yoke.

What does it mean to escape an "unequal" yoke (verse 17)?

What the Bible is saying adds up to this: Run away from evil. What's the promise God makes to you when you live like one of God's holy people (verse 18)?

INSIGHT Ditching evil doesn't *make* you a Christian, but wising up does allow you to *experience* life as God's daughter or son. You have God's acceptance, but standing clear of sin is the only way to enjoy closeness to him.

BIG QUESTIONS What sorts of relationships "yoke" you?

Tell what you think this Bible Chunk is saying:

It's okay to have non-Christian friends	OK	Not OK
It's okay to have close non-Christian friends	OK	Not OK
It's okay to have a non-Christian best friend	OK	Not OK
It's okay to have a non-Christian boyfriend or girlfriend	OK	Not OK
It's okay to pick a non-Christian spouse	OK	Not OK

Where did you draw the line of "not okay"? Why did you draw it where you did?

SIDELIGHT You can't cut off friends who need to be pulled toward God, or you would be cutting yourself off from God's purpose to tell the world about him. But the whole point of not being yoked is that sometimes you have to put some distance between you and people who pull you in the wrong direction. The closer and bigger the relationship, the better the chance it will control you. If you have to wonder whether a relationship is bad for you, mull this: It probably is.

What do your best friends do to pull you closer to Jesus?

What do your best friends do that hurts your closeness to God?

If Jesus were pulling you one way and your friends were pulling you another, who would win? How do you know?

DEEP THOT You've maybe heard this Bible Chunk applied to guy-girl relationships—and it absolutely applies to that. But it's also way bigger than that. One tip: Only when you're tightly tied to Jesus can you befriend nonbelievers without getting pulled off where you know you shouldn't go. And that's no yoke.

STICKY STUFF Hook up with 2 Corinthians 6:14 and never let go.

ACT ON IT Ask a mature Christian if he or she sees any of your relationships or commitments endangering your spiritual health. If they are, what are you going to do about it?

DIG ON Read 2 Timothy 2:20–22, where Paul tells Timothy how to pick friends that pull him toward God.

20. Crazy Huge Thing Called Love
God's plan for love and sex

The guys just wouldn't shut up about how Caleb had "never done anything" with a girl. Caleb wasn't shy. He wasn't ugly. But he was starting to wonder what he was waiting for. Maybe up until now it was his parents' bluntly reminding him that sex and the stuff that leads up to it were things you save for marriage. Or his youth pastor telling horror stories about students who'd gotten into trouble. Or his health teacher scaring him with the big odds his bod would contract a whole zoo of mutant STDs. Whatever it was or wasn't that had held him back until now, Caleb was starting to waffle. . . .

BRAIN DRAIN What do you think about saving sex for marriage? Why do you think that way? How much does your faith impact your choice?

FLASHBACK Sex wasn't invented yesterday. If you ever wonder whether the Bible has anything up-to-date to say about sexuality, ponder what was going on when it was written. Believers were surrounded by people who made sex a religious rite—and staffed temples with prostitutes for so-called worship. Early Christians came out of huge sexual sin, including affairs, incest, premarital sex, and homosexuality. So when you're trying to wise up in your guy-girl relationships, the Bible has loads to tell you. This Bible Chunk is one of the biggies on the topic.

BIBLE CHUNK Read 1 Thessalonians 4:1–8

(1) Finally, brothers, we instructed you how to live in order to please God, as in fact you are living. Now we ask you and urge you in the Lord

Jesus to do this more and more. (2) For you know what instructions we gave you by the authority of the Lord Jesus. (3) It is God's will that you should be sanctified: that you should avoid sexual immorality; (4) that each of you should learn to control his own body in a way that is holy and honorable, (5) not in passionate lust like the heathen, who do not know God; (6) and that in this matter no one should wrong his brother or take advantage of him. The Lord will punish men for all such sins, as we have already told you and warned you. (7) For God did not call us to be impure, but to live a holy life. (8) Therefore, he who rejects this instruction does not reject man but God, who gives you his Holy Spirit.

STUFF TO KNOW What does it mean to "please God" (verse 1)?

SIDELIGHT The fact that God loves you just as you are is one of the Bible's most astounding truths. Look at the best-known Bible verse on this topic, Romans 5:8: "But God demonstrates his own love for us in this: While we were still sinners, Christ died for us." You can't please God in the sense of earning his favor or love. But you bring him joy when you live like he commands. You display the smartness of his ways, and you experience the coolness of his closeness.

"Sanctified" is a whopper big word—but what do you think it means in this Bible Chunk (verse 3)?

DA'SCOOP The Bible calls what happens when you first trust in Jesus "justification." God declares you not guilty of your sins because of Jesus' death on your behalf. "Sanctification" is all the growth that happens after that. To "sanctify" means to "make holy," to "dedicate to God," to "set apart." Sanctification is the process of wising up and standing clear of the unsmartness of sin. So when you are sanctified, you increasingly live for God.

So what are you supposed to avoid? What are you supposed to control (verses 3–4)?

SIDELIGHT "Control his own body" can also be translated as "live with his own wife" or "acquire a wife." The point is the same: What the Bible calls "sexual immorality" is way out of bounds. Way back toward the beginning of the Old Testament God uttered the command that "you shall not commit adultery" (Exodus 20:14)—have sexual relations outside of marriage. Sexual immorality means more than that, including sex *before* marriage and all other types of sexual sin.

What does controlling your body look like (verse 4)? What is it not (verse 5)?

DA'SCOOP "Lust" is sinful desire, wanting something you can't have. See what Jesus says about it in Matthew 5:27–30.

So why not engage in sexual immorality? Look for reason 1: What's the impact on other people? And reason 2: What's the consequence God promises (verse 6)?

INSIGHT With words like "brother," "his body," and "men" running all through this Bible Chunk, maybe you think Scripture just picks on hormonally crazy males. Other Bible Chunks recognize that women can be just as hot and bothersome. Proverbs, for example, warns guys against women whose lips "drip honey" yet are as "sharp as a double-edged sword" (Proverbs 5:3–4).

Who thunk up this command? If you ditch this teaching, who are you rejecting (verse 8)?

BIG QUESTIONS Do you think God makes commands about sex just to ruin everyone's fun? Argue why or why not.

Here are your two options: You can (a) follow the cravings of your body and emotions as interpreted by your hormonally overcharged brain, or (b) follow God's commands, which are meant to channel those God-given desires into a healthy, happy life. Which do you want to follow?

Suppose you want to make God's good choice to stay sexually pure, both before and within marriage. What human being is helping you stick to that choice?

DEEP THOT If you bounce from bed to bed or leap from lips to lips, you'll never fill the craving for deep human love that God built into your heart. Wise up to this one: "Marriage should be honored by everyone, and husband and wife should keep their marriage pure. God will judge as guilty those who take part in sexual sins" (Hebrews 13:4 NCV).

STICKY STUFF You'll love living your love life according to 1 Thessalonians 4:3–4.

ACT ON IT What plan do you have to stay pure? Write yourself a letter as a reminder of your commitment. Put it someplace where you'll see it.

DIG ON Read Proverbs 5:15–23 for God's great idea of married love.

Talk About It • 4

EMPATHIZE: What's going on in your life?
ENCOURAGE: How are you doing with Jesus?
EQUIP: What one truth will you take home today?

- What does God have to do with your getting along with your parents? (Study 16)
- How do you struggle with your parents? How do you suppose they struggle with you? (Study 16)
- Who is someone in charge of some part of your life that you have a hard time submitting to? So why submit—or not? (Study 17)
- How do you react when a friend or foe goes cruel all over you? Do you hold back—or hit back? (Study 18)
- Why is blessing your enemies like barbecuing their brains? (Study 18)
- Who is your closest friend? What makes him or her so near and dear? (Study 19)
- What's it mean to be wrongly "yoked"?

It's okay to have non-Christian friends	OK	Not OK
It's okay to have close non-Christian friends	OK	Not OK
It's okay to have a non-Christian best friend	OK	Not OK
It's okay to have a non-Christian boyfriend or girlfriend	OK	Not OK
It's okay to pick a non-Christian spouse	OK	Not OK

- What do you think about saving sex for marriage? (Study 20)
- Why not give in to sexual immorality? (Study 20)

STANDING UP TO SIN

21. Stand Tall
Be all that God made you to be

"I grew up in a mean neighborhood during the Great Depression," Marc's grandpa said as they walked. "We didn't have much. Everyone on my block became a cop or a crook. I had plenty of chances to go wrong. But I didn't want to disappoint my parents. They believed in me. I figured that if they had that much trust in me, I needed to respect myself and the boundaries they set for me. I wanted to live up to their expectations. I've wanted to keep that trust all my life."

BRAIN DRAIN Who believes in you—that you can be a spiritual success?

FLASHBACK If people looked down on you long enough and told you you'll never amount to much, sooner or later you'd probably believe them. But when someone believes in your real abilities and potential, there's no telling what you can do. Peter told the people who got his letter that they had nothing less than the power of Christ's resurrection rearranging their lives (1 Peter 1:3). They were becoming nothing short of a magnificent living temple to God (2:4–6). And they *already* had become God's very own people.

Peter urged his readers to live up to their high calling. "As obedient children," he wrote, "do not conform to the evil desires you had when you lived in ignorance. But just as he who called you is holy, so be holy in all you do" (1 Peter 1:14–15). And you know what? God is doing the same grand stuff in you.

BIBLE CHUNK Read 1 Peter 2:9–12

(9) But you are a chosen people, a royal priesthood, a holy nation, a people belonging to God, that you may declare the praises of him who called you out of darkness into his wonderful light. (10) Once you were not a people, but now you are the people of God; once you had not received mercy, but now you have received mercy.

(11) Dear friends, I urge you, as aliens and strangers in the world, to abstain from sinful desires, which war against your soul. (12) Live such good lives among the pagans that, though they accuse you of doing wrong, they may see your good deeds and glorify God on the day he visits us.

STUFF TO KNOW Right off the bat this Bible Chunk says that you—along with a great crowd of Christans—are four things. Yep, *you*. So what are you (verse 9)?

Now that you're all that, what are you to do (verse 9)?

What are you now that you weren't before? What have you gotten that you didn't have before (verse 10)?

DA'SCOOP You're a "chosen people" (hand-picked by God). A "royal priesthood" (equipped to serve and worship your king). A "holy nation" (dedicated to his purposes). And never forget this one: a "people belonging to God" (God's very own family).

INSIGHT You might read that Bible snippet and snidely think that God just wants to dress you up as a walking, talking billboard advertising his greatness. But God has given you something even more priceless than an hour of Super Bowl ad time. You're one of God's own. You bask in his light. You roll in his mercy. You can tell others how they can belong to God too. That's worth talking up!

Here's the weird part. You're incredibly special, but what two sort-of-ugly names does Peter call you in verse 11?

SIDELIGHT Alien? Stranger? That's what you are, but not because you're some alien life-form. Your real home is heaven (see John 14:1–4 and Phillipians 3:20). And Hebrews says this about some great women and men of faith: "They admitted that they were aliens and strangers on earth. . . . They were longing for a better country—a heavenly one" (11:13, 16).

By this point in *Wise Up* you know that when you follow Jesus, you ditch sin. This Bible Chunk offers a reason to run from evil that we haven't run across before. What do sinful desires do to your soul (verse 11)?

INSIGHT Letting evil desires go on living inside you puts your soul in deadly danger. It's like begging to get shot at. Or torched with a flamethrower. Or blown up by a tank.

When people look at you, they might miss your identity as a child of the King of the Universe. Some of them might think you're just an alien. Or even an evildoer. But who will be proven right in the end (verse 12)?

BIG QUESTIONS What does it matter to you that you're one of God's own people?

What good does it do you to have received God's mercy?

So what would you tell someone who asked what God has done for you?

Knowing that you have gargantuan gifts and possibilities, how do you want to live?

DEEP THOT When something inside you wants to live less-than-wisely, remember who Jesus has made you. Recall the great things God has done for you. And if you're really all that, stand up and live like it.

STICKY STUFF Think deep thoughts about what God has done for you by tucking 1 Peter 2:9 away in your brain.

ACT ON IT No son or daughter likes to hear a parent say, "You're not living up to your potential." But think of things where you're maybe living less-than-best. Do you really want to settle for that when God made you for something so much better?

DIG ON Read in Revelation 21:1–8 a bit more about your royal destiny as part of God's people.

22. The Devil Didn't Make You Do It

Where temptation comes from

You know you're short on cash, but you still take the shirt into the dressing room for a try-on. And just like you suspected—it's no contest the coolest clothing ever to be on your bod. You're weeks away from having enough allowance to pay the absurd amount on the price tag. Yet you've dreamed so much about getting the shirt that everyone else at school is wearing that you're convinced you've got to get it now. As you change back into your clothes you wrap the shirt around your leg, under your pants. And you shuffle out of the store.

BRAIN DRAIN Even if you're not into shoplifting shirts, why do you suppose you experience temptation to do stuff you know you shouldn't?

FLASHBACK Several people named James pop up in the New Testament, but the author of this Bible Chunk happened to be the brother of Jesus and chief leader of the church in Jerusalem. He wrote to Jewish Christians scattered across the Roman Empire to help them make faith work in real life. He began his letter with this bang: "Consider it pure joy. . . whenever you face trials of many kinds," he wrote, "because you know that the testing of your faith develops perseverance" (James 1:2–3). Just because you wise up doesn't mean life always goes smoothly. And just because you want to stand clear of the unsmartness of sin doesn't mean doing wrong never looks attractive.

BIBLE CHUNK Read James 1:12–18

(12) Blessed is the man who perseveres under trial, because when he has stood the test, he will receive the crown of life that God has promised to those who love him.

(13) When tempted, no one should say, "God is tempting me." For God cannot be tempted by evil, nor does he tempt anyone; (14) but each one is tempted when, by his own evil desire, he is dragged away and enticed. (15) Then, after desire has conceived, it gives birth to sin; and sin, when it is full-grown, gives birth to death.

(16) Don't be deceived, my dear brothers. (17) Every good and perfect gift is from above, coming down from the Father of the heavenly lights, who does not change like shifting shadows. (18) He chose to give us birth through the word of truth, that we might be a kind of firstfruits of all he created.

STUFF TO KNOW Why be happy when life gets tough (verse 12)?

What do you receive when you survive life's tests (verse 12)?

DA'SCOOP The words for "to stand the test" were used of a coin that had been pounded and proven genuine. The "crown of life" here isn't eternal life, because you can't earn that. It's the crown given to an athlete—a wreath of laurel, oak, or even celery—to symbolize victory and the good life that comes from living close to God.

There's something you're not supposed to whine about when you're tempted. Who can't you blame (verse 13)?

Jump ahead a few verses—and get clear on this, because James says outright that he doesn't want you duped. How do you know God wouldn't tempt you (verse 17)?

INSIGHT Maybe you picture God sitting up in heaven flicking temptations your way like a five-year-old putting twigs in the path of an ant. That won't happen. God is wholly against sin. He doesn't engineer circumstances to egg you on or in any way invite you to sin. Without variation, God's gifts are unchangingly kind and helpful—not destructive.

According to this Bible Chunk, what drags you off and makes you itch for evil (verse 14)?

INSIGHT It would be a cinch to blame someone or something else when you're tempted, like "the devil made me do it." But note where James lays blame. You can almost smell your own fiendish desire rising out of a stinking grave to grab you by the hair and drag you off. Fill in the blank:

- Evil desire gives birth to an ugly kid called _____.
- Sin gives birth to an even uglier kid called _____.

BIG QUESTIONS What temptations do you face that turn your life into a test—say, a mildly unpleasant pop-quiz kind of test?

What temptations do you face that turn your life into a you-think-you're-gonna-die, you-don't-know-how-you're-gonna-survive kind of test?

So when you feel tempted to sin, what would this Bible Chunk say is the first thing you need to fix?

If *you* are the big reason you feel temptation, what does that say about how you should attack it?

Do you see temptation as an opportunity to grow up—or to give up and get dragged away?

SIDELIGHT As strong as it sounds in this Bible Chunk that temptation is all your fault, James knew that there's more to temptation than that. Temptation is something that wells up from within, but sometimes it's also like you're getting pelted with rocks and garbage from the outside. More on that in the next study, but read what James wrote later in his letter: "Submit yourselves, then, to God. Resist the devil, and he will flee from you" (James 4:7).

DEEP THOT Life as a Christian isn't just the grand stuff of being God's people. You won't wise up without knowing how to steer through stubborn temptations.

STICKY STUFF Mull deeply the point James 1:14 makes about temptation.

ACT ON IT Today when you get hit hard with a temptation to do wrong, think about how your own desires keep you wanting what you shouldn't. Ask the God who gives good gifts to help you stand.

DIG ON Read James 4:7–10 for the rest of what James says later in his letter about temptation.

23. To Sin or to Win
The full armor of God

People had always told Kirsti that when you worked a cash register you forgot you were handling money. "Money's just paper," they'd say. Kirsti wished it was that easy. She thought of all the things she'd buy if she could siphon money out of the drawer without being noticed. But it wasn't until someone told her how to do it that the temptation became overwhelming. . . .

BRAIN DRAIN When have you caved in to someone pestering you to do wrong?

FLASHBACK The devil doesn't make you sin. But he and his henchmen sure spend a lot of time selling you on the idea. Here's how you know: James said you need to "resist the devil" (James 4:7). Peter said that "Your enemy the devil prowls around like a roaring lion looking for someone to devour" (1 Peter 5:8). And the devil himself showed up to tempt Jesus face-to-face at the start of Jesus' public ministry (Matthew 4:1–11). Temptation feeds on desires that form on your insides. But it sure doesn't help that evil is often egged on from the outside. The last Bible Chunk you read focused on misguided desires. This one brings to light the outward fight.

BIBLE CHUNK Read Ephesians 6:10–18

(10) Finally, be strong in the Lord and in his mighty power. (11) Put on the full armor of God so that you can take your stand against the devil's schemes. (12) For our struggle is not against flesh and blood, but against

the rulers, against the authorities, against the powers of this dark world and against the spiritual forces of evil in the heavenly realms. (13) Therefore put on the full armor of God, so that when the day of evil comes, you may be able to stand your ground, and after you have done everything, to stand. (14) Stand firm then, with the belt of truth buckled around your waist, with the breastplate of righteousness in place, (15) and with your feet fitted with the readiness that comes from the gospel of peace. (16) In addition to all this, take up the shield of faith, with which you can extinguish all the flaming arrows of the evil one. (17) Take the helmet of salvation and the sword of the Spirit, which is the word of God. (18) And pray in the Spirit on all occasions with all kinds of prayers and requests. With this in mind, be alert and always keep on praying for all the saints.

STUFF TO KNOW Where do you go to get strong (verse 10)?

If your struggle isn't against flesh and blood—people—who exactly do you square off against (verse 12)?

DA'SCOOP Each of the beings mentioned here—rulers, authorities, powers of this dark world, and spiritual forces of evil in the heavenly realm—is not a human opponent but an evil spiritual power. The Bible teaches that Satan is an angel created by God who rebelled against God's authority, led other angels to do the same, and now encourages the human race to rise up against God. You might have a hard time imagining the devil and his hellish demon friends being behind every temptation you face—say, to belt your little brother. But the Bible calls him "the ruler of the kingdom of the air, the spirit who is now at work in those who are disobedient" (Ephesians 2:2).

If those are the forces wanting to thump you good, how do you get ready to fight (verses 11, 13)?

What kind of outcome does Paul expect when evil takes a whack at you? Does he expect you to win—or to sin (verse 13)?

INSIGHT Paul used everyday military language to paint his picture of the "full armor of God," which gives clues of what he had in mind. Belts were more than decoration; they hoisted a soldier's tunic and made him ready for action. Breastplates covered vital organs from neck to thigh, and here the protection is provided by "righteousness," or character. A soldier's boots were made of thick leather studded with nails for traction and speed. (Believe it or not, good shoes were that day's weapon of mass destruction and brought decisive victories to the armies of Alexander the Great.) Shields could come back from battle stuck full of dozens of darts. Helmets were actually handed to soldiers by their armor-bearers—not something they picked up themselves. That's a great picture of God's gift of salvation and how it protects your head. And the specific sword named by Paul was a short, maneuverable offensive weapon.

Think hard about these. What does each piece of armor do? What kind of threat does each protect you against (verses 14–17)?

- belt of truth

- breastplate of righteousness

- feet fitted with the readiness that comes from the gospel of peace

- shield of faith

- helmet of salvation

- sword of the Spirit

What else do you need to do in the devil's schemes (verse 18)?

DA'SCOOP To "pray in the Spirit" means both to stick

close to the Spirit's desires and to pray in the Spirit's power.

BIG QUESTIONS How do you feel pressures bigger than your own less-than-best desires influencing your choices?

When you feel walloped by temptation, do you expect to win or to sin? Why?

SIDELIGHT Colossians 2:15 says that at the cross, Jesus "disarmed the powers and authorities" and "made a public spectacle of them, triumphing over them." Satan fights on, but his defeat is sure. He will be completely disempowered at the end of time (Revelation 20:10).

DEEP THOT You don't have to sin. Putting on God's full armor allows you to win.

STICKY STUFF Get ready for battle with Ephesians 6:10–11 as ammo for your brain.

ACT ON IT Ask a mature Christian how he or she battles temptation. What works? What doesn't?

DIG ON Flip to Matthew 4:1–11 to see for yourself how Jesus used Scripture to stand up to Satan's temptations.

(24.) Famous Last Words
Standing up to temptation

As a little kid Ryan watched his dad get drunk and beat up his mom. So when Ryan got old enough to think about it, he swore he would never have a problem with alcohol. After all, he had all the reasons in the world not to get hammered, and he thought he was too close to God to get sucked in to sin. But when his friends kept offering him beer, Ryan found out he was wrong.

BRAIN DRAIN What do you think the chances are that at some time in your Christian life you will take a tumble—or suffer a major crash and burn? What will keep that from happening?

FLASHBACK This Bible Chunk starts with a tale of God's Old Testament people. Paul detailed all their one-of-a-kind spiritual experiences—but then showed that what those people knew about God never made a difference in their lives. If you want to translate their story into your world, think of it like this: They joined the right church. They went to youth group. They attended Bible study. They sang loudly in worship. They met with a small group. They were given wisdom and had the power at their disposal to live out that wisdom. But they still got slammed by sin. In this Bible Chunk you get the how and why.

BIBLE CHUNK Read 1 Corinthians 10:1–13

(1) For I do not want you to be ignorant of the fact, brothers, that our forefathers were all under the cloud and that they all passed through the sea. (2) They were all baptized into Moses in the cloud and in the sea. (3)

They all ate the same spiritual food (4) and drank the same spiritual drink; for they drank from the spiritual rock that accompanied them, and that rock was Christ. (5) Nevertheless, God was not pleased with most of them; their bodies were scattered over the desert.

(6) Now these things occurred as examples to keep us from setting our hearts on evil things as they did. (7) Do not be idolaters, as some of them were; as it is written: "The people sat down to eat and drink and got up to indulge in pagan revelry." (8) We should not commit sexual immorality, as some of them did—and in one day twenty-three thousand of them died. (9) We should not test the Lord, as some of them did—and were killed by snakes. (10) And do not grumble, as some of them did—and were killed by the destroying angel.

(11) These things happened to them as examples and were written down as warnings for us, on whom the fulfillment of the ages has come. (12) So, if you think you are standing firm, be careful that you don't fall! (13) No temptation has seized you except what is common to man. And God is faithful; he will not let you be tempted beyond what you can bear. But when you are tempted, he will also provide a way out so that you can stand up under it.

STUFF TO KNOW Without diving into too-deep detail, "under the cloud" means God's Old Testament people all experienced his guidance. "Through the sea" says they all gained freedom from slavery when God jammed his hand into Egyptian history. "Baptized into Moses" means they were all united to God via one of God's right-hand leaders. And through all of this they even experienced Christ.

After getting all those benefits, what did God think of them? And what happened to them (verse 5)?

So why did they wipe out? (Hint: Look at the second half of verse 6.)

What sins were they guilty of (verses 7–10)?

INSIGHT Sparing the ugly details, these folks were into idol-

atry, or worshiping other gods—remember the golden calf? (Exodus 32:1–6); pagan celebrations (Exodus 32:6); sexual immorality, which led to 23,000 deaths (Numbers 25:1–9); testing God, to which God responded with poisonous snakes (Numbers 21:6); and grumbling, which brought on a plague of death (Numbers 14:2, 37).

Hmm . . . what good can their gory story do you (verse 11)?

What's the big warning their situation screams (verse 12)?

INSIGHT The Israelites assumed they were above temptation. Watch out when you utter what might become your famous last words before you fall into sin: "That could never happen to me." "That's so horrible I'd never do it." "I'm strong. I can handle this." "I don't feel tempted at all." "I'm spiritual in the rest of life. It's okay if I do this one little thing."

After all this nasty news, in verse 13 God makes a three-part promise. Answer these quickies:

- Are you the first one to feel tempted?

- Will a temptation ever be too big to resist?

- What will God provide for you when you're tempted?

BIG QUESTIONS When this Bible Chunk says you can't suffer a temptation that isn't "common to man," here's a clearer version of what it means: "The temptations that come into your life are no different from what others experience." And here's the rest: God will "keep the temptation from becoming so strong that you can't stand up against it." And he will "show you a way out so that you will not give in to it" (1 Corinthians 10:13 NLT).

Think of the biggest temptation you face. Do you think it's too big to overcome? Why or why not?

Think of that same whopper temptation. What ways of escape has God provided for you?

DEEP THOT Being tempted is unavoidable. Being overwhelmed is not. When you feel tempted, know that you've got a God who understands: "For we do not have a high priest who is unable to sympathize with our weaknesses, but we have one who has been tempted in every way, just as we are—yet was without sin. Let us then approach the throne of grace with confidence, so that we may receive mercy and find grace to help us in our time of need" (Hebrews 4:15–16).

STICKY STUFF You've always got a way out, and 1 Corinthians 10:13 will help you remember it.

ACT ON IT Dig deep into your brain and try to recall any time you've uttered any of those famous last words on the previous page.

DIG ON Do a double take and reread 1 Corinthians 12:12 if you've ever thought you've wised up past any danger of being sucked away from God.

25. Ride Hard
Pressing on in faith

You're a long way out from the end of the cycling race, but still you can smell the finish line. You're in a pace line, drafting your team-mates, taking turns at the lead so everyone whomps the ride. You know that if you keep your brain engaged, you'll zing together through the finish line. But if you don't, well, you could touch tires with another rider and end up in a mash of twisted metal and body parts . . . or you might run out of energy and have to whine your way to the end . . . or you could drift off the side of the road and wind up a walking pile of shredded skin toting your broken bike on your shoulder . . . or . . . Well, you'd just rather stay focused.

BRAIN DRAIN Why not just give in to sin? What makes winning against temptation important to you?

FLASHBACK The book of Hebrews begins with a cosmi-cally huge description of who Jesus is and what he came to accom-plish. "The Son," Hebrews says, "is the radiance of God's glory" and he "provided purification for sins" (Hebrews 1:3). It quickly nails why Jesus came with this practical point: "See to it . . . that none of you has a sinful, unbelieving heart that turns away from the living God" (3:12). And just before the Bible Chunk you'll read, Hebrews presents its "Hall of Faith," a chapter chock-full of people who got to know their great Lord and followed him faithfully. They're the "witnesses" in heaven who now "surround" us and watch us run the race of faith.

BIBLE CHUNK Read Hebrews 12:1–13

(1) Therefore, since we are surrounded by such a great cloud of witnesses, let us throw off everything that hinders and the sin that so easily entangles, and let us run with perseverance the race marked out for us. (2) Let us fix our eyes on Jesus, the author and perfecter of our faith, who for the joy set before him endured the cross, scorning its shame, and sat down at the right hand of the throne of God. (3) Consider him who endured such opposition from sinful men, so that you will not grow weary and lose heart.

(4) In your struggle against sin, you have not yet resisted to the point of shedding your blood. (5) And you have forgotten that word of encouragement that addresses you as sons:
"My son, do not make light of the Lord's discipline,
and do not lose heart when he rebukes you,
(6) because the Lord disciplines those he loves,
and he punishes everyone he accepts as a son."

(7) Endure hardship as discipline; God is treating you as sons. For what son is not disciplined by his father? (8) If you are not disciplined (and everyone undergoes discipline), then you are illegitimate children and not true sons. (9) Moreover, we have all had human fathers who disciplined us and we respected them for it. How much more should we submit to the Father of our spirits and live! (10) Our fathers disciplined us for a little while as they thought best; but God disciplines us for our good, that we may share in his holiness. (11) No discipline seems pleasant at the time, but painful. Later on, however, it produces a harvest of righteousness and peace for those who have been trained by it.

(12) Therefore, strengthen your feeble arms and weak knees. (13) Make level paths for your feet," so that the lame may not be disabled, but rather healed.

STUFF TO KNOW If you were running a race, why would you want to throw off everything that "hinders" or "entangles" you? What would that enable you to do (verse 1)?

INSIGHT There are two different ideas here. Things that "hinder" aren't wrong in themselves, but they get in the way of your all-out effort. The "sin that so easily entangles," on the other hand, inevitably sends you sprawling. One other thing: Notice this race is way more than a sprint. It's a long-distance race that can only be done with concentration and determination.

How did Jesus view the cross—the incredibly painful thing that stood between him and the finish line (verse 2)?

What good could it possibly do to "fix your eyes on Jesus," thinking of him as your example? Isn't he totally unlike you (verses 2–3)?

Okay. Wising up and standing clear of sin's unsmartness is hard work. But it could be worse. What haven't you suffered yet (verse 4)?

What's so encouraging about the words in verses 5–8? What's this Bible Chunk saying about how you should look at the tough race of faith?

INSIGHT Here's some hot news: Suffering doesn't have to be accidental misery. God uses what you go through to make you more like him. If you're God's child, he disciplines you. If you aren't disciplined, then you aren't really his kid.

What's the difference between the discipline of parents and the discipline of God (verse 10)?

BIG QUESTIONS What does discipline feel like?

What does discipline produce? (Peek back at verse 11.)

INSIGHT God's work in your life is unlike any other. It produces a whole heap of "righteousness" (a healthy habit of life—good actions) and "peace" (a godly attitude). That sounds blessedly happy, like what you heard about when you first cracked open this book.

How are you hoping to keep growing now that you've finished *Wise Up*? What's your plan?

INSIGHT Verses 12 and 13 of this Bible Chunk have a couple good ideas: (1) Keep training your weak points, and (2) keep learning how to spot God's best path for your life.

DEEP THOT Human discipline often works by threats, forcing your outsides to behave even while your insides can't sit still. God disciplines you to help you understand, reworking you from the inside out. He knows that when you wise up his way, he won't have to convince you it's a good idea to stand clear of the unsmartness of sin. You'll follow him becuase you want to.

STICKY STUFF Hebrews 12:1–2 is one thing to carry with you even when you're running light.

ACT ON IT Make sure you have a plan to keep getting closer to Jesus. Do the first step of your plan today.

DIG ON Read Hebrews 11 to find out about people who stuck tight with God.

Talk About It • 5

EMPATHIZE: What's going on in your life?
ENCOURAGE: How are you doing with Jesus?
EQUIP: What one truth will you take home today?

- Who believes in you—that you can be a spiritual success? (Study 21)
- What does it matter to you that you are a "chosen people," a "royal priesthood," a "holy nation," a "people belonging to God"? (Study 21)
- What would you tell someone who asked what God has done for you? (Study 21)
- What causes temptation? (Studies 22 and 23)
- What does James 1:14 say drags you off and makes you itch for evil? Do you think James is right? (Study 22)
- When you feel tempted to sin, what is the first thing you need to fix? (Study 22)
- Does the devil make you sin? (Study 23)
- What trouble does the devil cause you? (Study 23)
- How can you arm yourself against "the devil's schemes"? (Study 23)
- What do you think the chances are that at some time in your Christian life you will take a tumble—or suffer a major crash and burn? What will keep that from happening? (Study 24)
- What three-part promise does God make you in 1 Corinthians 10:13? How will that help you through life? (Study 24)
- How does Jesus encourage you in your battle to stick close to God? (Study 25)
- What's your plan to keep growing now that you're done with *Wise Up*?

STRAIGHT TALK

peer pressure★school

BOOKS FOR YOUR GROWING FAITH

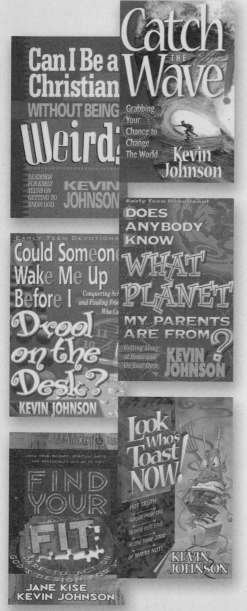

CAN I BE A CHRISTIAN WITHOUT BEING WEIRD?
A series of devotional readings to excite young teens to make Bible reading and prayer a habit by making Scripture understandable and relevant.

CATCH THE WAVE!
An engaging guide to involve teens with God's work in the world. Explores how prayer, ministry at church, school, and around the world can be used by teens to discover the bigness of God's plan.

COULD SOMEBODY WAKE ME UP BEFORE I DROOL ON THE DESK?
Addressing the ups and downs of school and the need to find friends who count, this collection of devotions will point young teens to God as they navigate the tricky path through middle school and beyond.

DOES ANYBODY KNOW WHAT PLANET MY PARENTS ARE FROM?
A fresh look at the homelife of early teens, this collection of readings explores how young adults can make friends at home, walk smart when their parents aren't around, and choose to follow Jesus.

FIND YOUR FIT
Based on the LifeKeys guides to self-discovery, this book provides interactive questions, inventories, and exercises for teens to better understand their talents, skills, and spiritual gifts as they look toward the future.

LOOK WHO'S TOAST NOW!
Answers for teens' insatiable curiosity about the future—the end of the world, death, hell, and Satan. Provides the hope that teens need in this chaotic world and motivation to live holy, patient lives now.

FROM KEVIN JOHNSON

So Who Says I Have to Act My Age?
Written in acknowledgment that young teens are often caught between being kids and being adults, this group of devotions helps readers understand the inevitable changes that come with growing up.

Was That a Balloon or Did Your Head Just Pop?
A collection of 45 readings that provides the tools for early teens to break free from peer fear, get past put-downs and crowd control, find real popularity with God, and grow into a friend worth having.

What's With the Dudes at the Door?
A revealing and alerting teen-friendly look at the major cults. An invaluable tool that provides biblical answers to the key teachings of Mormonism, Jehovah's Witnesses, and other major cults.

Who Should I Listen To?
This group of readings helps early teens hear God's voice about the pressure-packed roar of the world and gives biblical wisdom to guide them in discerning truth from lies.

Why Can't My Life Be a Summer Vacation?
Addressing problems both major and minor—broken friendships to bad hair days—this collection of readings teaches early teens that God provides patient support to help them attain what He has planned for them.

Why Is God Looking for Friends?
In the language of young teens, this book examines and affirms their longing for friendships that reflects the core of our human nature as God created us.

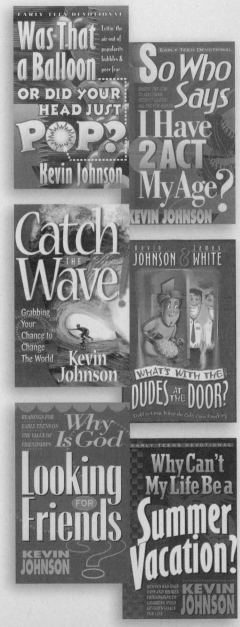

WISE UP 5
Getting to know God remakes you

Titus 3:4–5

But when the kindness and love of God
our Savior appeared, he saved us, not
because of righteous things we had done,
but because of his mercy. He saved us
through the washing of rebirth and
renewal by the Holy Spirit.

WISE UP 1
Wanting God's wise way

Proverbs 2:6

For the Lord gives wisdom,
and from his mouth
come knowledge and understanding.

WISE UP 6
God scrubs you from the inside out

Ephesians 4:22–24

You were taught . . . to be made new in
the attitude of your minds; and to put on
the new self, created to be like God in true
righteousness and holiness.

WISE UP 2
Sticking close to God

Psalm 1:1–2

Blessed is the man who does not walk in
the counsel of the wicked or stand in the
way of sinners or sit in the seat of
mockers. But his delight is in the law of
the Lord, and on his law he meditates
day and night.

WISE UP 7
God's power to change

2 Peter 1:3

His divine power has given us everything
we need for life and godliness through
our knowledge of him who called us by
his own glory and goodness.

WISE UP 3
God's flawless wisdom

Psalm 19:7

The law of the Lord is perfect,
reviving the soul.
The statutes of the Lord are trustworthy,
making wise the simple.

WISE UP 8
The Spirit grows fruit in you

Galatians 5:22–23

But the fruit of the Spirit is love, joy, peace,
patience, kindness, goodness, faithfulness,
gentleness and self-control. Against such
things there is no law.

WISE UP 4
Wising up changes how you live

Ephesians 5:15

Be very careful, then, how you live—
not as unwise but as wise.

Hanging on to Christ's humility

Philippians 2:4–5

Each of you should look not only to your own interests, but also to the interests of others. Your attitude should be the same as that of Christ Jesus.

Getting up and growing on

Philippians 3:13b–14

But one thing I do: Forgetting what is behind and straining toward what is ahead, I press on toward the goal to win the prize for which God has called me heavenward in Christ Jesus.

Get filled up with God

Matthew 6:33

But seek first his kingdom and his righteousness, and all these things will be given to you as well.

God won't ever stop working in you

Philippians 1:6

Being confident of this, that he who began a good work in you will carry it on to completion until the day of Christ Jesus.

Owning up to God

Matthew 10:32

Whoever acknowledges me before men, I will also acknowledge him before my Father in heaven.

Grace teaches you to say "No!"

Titus 2:11–12

For the grace of God that brings salvation has appeared to all men. It teaches us to say "No" to ungodliness and worldly passions, and to live self-controlled, upright and godly lives in this present age.

Getting along at home

Ephesians 6:1

Children, obey your parents in the Lord, for this is right.

There's nothing better than being you

Psalm 139:14

I praise you because I am fearfully and wonderfully made; your works are wonderful, I know that full well.

Be all that God made you to be

1 Peter 2:9

But you are a chosen people, a royal priesthood, a holy nation, a people belonging to God, that you may declare the praises of him who called you out of darkness into his wonderful light.

Submitting to authority

Romans 13:1

Everyone must submit himself to the governing authorities, for there is no authority except that which God has established. The authorities that exist have been established by God.

Where temptation comes from

James 1:14

But each one is tempted when, by his own evil desire, he is dragged away and enticed.

Dealing with cruel people

Romans 12:19

Do not take revenge, my friends, but leave room for God's wrath, for it is written: "It is mine to avenge; I will repay," says the Lord.

The full armor of God

Ephesians 6:10–11

Finally, be strong in the Lord and in his mighty power. Put on the full armor of God so that you can take your stand against the devil's schemes.

Being tight with the right people

2 Corinthians 6:14

Do not be yoked together with unbelievers. For what do righteousness and wickedness have in common? Or what fellowship can light have with darkness?

Standing up to temptation

1 Corinthians 10:13

No temptation has seized you except what is common to man. And God is faithful; he will not let you be tempted beyond what you can bear. But when you are tempted, he will also provide a way out so that you can stand up under it.

God's plan for love and sex

1 Thessalonians 4:3–4

It is God's will that you should be sanctified: that you should avoid sexual immorality; that each of you should learn to control his own body in a way that is holy and honorable.

God promises to forgive you
1 John 1:8–9

If we claim to be without sin, we deceive ourselves and the truth is not in us. If we confess our sins, he is faithful and just and will forgive us our sins and purify us from all unrighteousness.

Pressing on in faith
Hebrews 12:1–2a

Let us throw off everything that hinders and the sin that so easily entangles, and let us run with perseverance the race marked out for us. Let us fix our eyes on Jesus, the author and perfecter of our faith.

God promises to forgive you
Psalm 103:11–12

For has high as the heavens are above the earth, so great is his love for those who fear him; as far as the east is from the west, so far has he removed our transgressions from us.

The source of smarts
Proverbs 1:7

The fear of the Lord is the beginning of knowledge, but fools despise wisdom and discipline.

Living for God
Romans 12:1

Therefore, I urge you, brothers, in view of God's mercy, to offer your bodies as living sacrifices, holy and pleasing to God—this is your spiritual act of worship.

The Bible's guidance
Psalm 119:105

Your word is a lamp to my feet and a light for my path.

Resisting the devil
James 4:7

Submit yourselves, then, to God. Resist the devil, and he will flee from you.

God's gracious love
Romans 5:8

But God demonstrates his own love for us in this: While we were still sinners, Christ died for us.